F*CK THIS JOURNAL

BETTERNESS THROUGH BITTERNESS

DALE SHAW

headline

COPYRIGHT © 2015 DALE SHAW

THE RIGHT OF DALE SHAW TO BE IDENTIFIED AS THE AUTHOR OF
THE WORK HAS BEEN ASSERTED BY HIM IN ACCORDANCE WITH THE
COPYRIGHT, DESIGNS AND PATENTS ACT 1988.

FIRST PUBLISHED IN 2015
BY HEADLINE PUBLISHING GROUP

1

CATALOGUING IN PUBLICATION DATA IS AVAILABLE FROM THE BRITISH LIBRARY

PAPERBACK ISBN 978 1 4722 3072 0
EBOOK ISBN 978 1 4722 3073 7

TYPESET IN DALESHAWHAND AND HANDLETTERED BY THE AUTHOR

PRINTED AND BOUND IN THE UK BY CLAYS LTD, ST IVES PLC

HEADLINE'S POLICY IS TO USE PAPERS THAT ARE NATURAL, RENEWABLE AND
RECYCLABLE PRODUCTS AND MADE FROM WOOD GROWN IN SUSTAINABLE FORESTS.
THE LOGGING AND MANUFACTURING PROCESSES ARE EXPECTED TO CONFORM
TO THE ENVIRONMENTAL REGULATIONS OF THE COUNTRY OF ORIGIN.

HEADLINE PUBLISHING GROUP
AN HACHETTE UK COMPANY
CARMELITE HOUSE
50 VICTORIA EMBANKMENT
LONDON EC4Y 0DZ

WWW.HEADLINE.CO.UK
WWW.HACHETTE.CO.UK

THIS BOOK IS DEDICATED TO ALL MY FELLOW MEMBERS OF THE ILLUMINATI WHO HAVE HELPED ME SO MUCH OVER THE YEARS. A LOVELY BUNCH OF LADS. DONALD, BILL, SIR ALAN, WARREN, RICHARD, DIDDY, RUPERT, PIERS, ALL THE GEORGES, ICKEY, CLARKO + STING.

THIS ONE'S FOR YOU!

INSTRUCTIONS!

Buy This Book!

Buy it Again!

Post A Positive Amazon Review!

(Five Stars - Not One of Those
'It's ok - Three Stars' Jobs)

(And Make Sure You're A Verified
Customer.)

Then Re-Register Under A Fake Name
And Add Another!

Oh, And HAVE FUN!

WHAT YOU WILL NEED!

▪ WELL IT'S A BOOK. LET'S SEE. WHAT DO YOU NORMALLY NEED WITH A BOOK?

▪ EYES? A MIND? LITERACY?

▪ HANDS I SUPPOSE? FOR HOLDING IT.

▪ I MEAN, DO YOU REALLY NEED TO BE TOLD WHAT YOU NEED?

▪ ARE YOU A CHILD?

▪ FRANKLY IF YOU'RE LOOKING FOR HELP IN HANDLING A BOOK, THIS MIGHT NOT BE FOR YOU.

▪ MAYBE RETURN IT AND BUY A PLANT OR SOMETHING.

▪ OR SOME COLOURED BALLS. JESUS.

HERE ARE SOME WORDS TO GET YOU STARTED!

BELLOWS! LEOPARD! STUMP!
NOSTRIL! LEBS! CHOKING!
QUINCE! BRIG! GINTY!
TRILLO! LAMP! STOBER!
MEXINE! CRANT! BUS!
WIBBED! LANDO! LRFO!
AARGIN! JBBB! VIDGE!
EALL! ENWP! CUBBRU!
BALZAC! PUP!

THINGS TO AVOID:
PARROT OWNERS
ANYONE IN A TABARD
CHEFS
DONKEYS
THE WORD 'HENCE'
ASSASSINS
CLOSED DOORS IN PUBLIC TOILETS
PEOPLE CALLED MITCH
EXPERTS
SLUGS
HAT WEARERS
POETS
CAROB

You can find inspiration anywhere! Even by simply writing the word 'inspiration.' Why don't you fill up the rest of this page by writing the word 'inspiration' as many times as you can! You'll be amazed how inspired you'll become!

YOU SEE? AREN'T YOU FILLED WITH INSPIRATION JUST BY WRITING THE WORD 'INSPIRATION' FOR THE SAKE OF INSPIRATION? OF COURSE YOU ARE! BUT IF YOU'RE NOT, JUST FILL THIS PAGE BY WRITING THE WORD 'INSPIRATION'. IT'S BOUND TO WORK THIS TIME!

NEED MORE INSPIRATION? LEARN FROM THE GREATS! LET'S ADOPT A TRICK FROM ERNEST HEMINGWAY. HE SAID, "WHEN I SEEK INSPIRATION I WRITE THE WORD 'INSPIRATION' OVER AND OVER AGAIN!" HEY! WHY NOT GIVE IT A TRY IN THE SPACE BELOW?

I AM A WRITER AND SO CAN YOU BE TOO !

"IF YOU GET STUCK JUST JAM AN URCHIN IN THERE. URCHINS ARE BRILLIANT. YOU CAN SHOVE THEM UP CHIMNEYS, HAVE THEM COUGH THEMSELVES TO DEATH OR JOIN A LARGE ROAMING GANG OF CRIMINALS LED BY A RACIALLY INSENSITIVE CULTURAL STEREOTYPE. HEY! THAT GIVES ME AN IDEA FOR A MUSICAL! YOU SEE? THIS SHIT WORKS! URCHINS!"

CHARLES "OLIVER" DICKENS

FREE PAGE!

FILL UP THIS PAGE WITH ANYTHING YOU FANCY! ANYTHING AT ALL! REALLY! I DON'T MIND! JUST LET YOUR IMAGINATION RUN WILD AND HURL IT ONTO THE BLANK SPACE BELOW. IT COULD BE A DRAWING. IT COULD BE A POEM, IT COULD BE A STORY ABOUT A HORNY DUCK! ANYTHING GOES! MERELY DIVE INTO YOUR CREATIVE RECESSES AND ADD THE RESULTING THOUGHTS TO THIS PAGE! IT'S AS EASY AS THAT! NO STRINGS ATTACHED! NONE! NOT A SINGLE ONE! IT'S ALL YOURS SO GO NUTS! OH.

COLOUR ME IN!
[DESPITE NOT BEING A CHILD!]
"NIC CAGE DRESSED AS A HOBO EATING A HAM AND CHEESE PANINI"

FILL IN YOUR ONLINE DATING PROFILE!

NAME _____

NAME EVERYONE KNOWS YOU
AS AT THE PETROL STATION

_____

AGE _____

ATTACH
PHOTO HERE ACTUAL
AGE _____

NUMBER OF TEETH _____

LEVEL OF CREEPINESS BETWEEN 1 + 10

_____

SUICIDE ATTEMPTS _____

NUMBER OF STING ALBUMS OWNED _____

HOW MANY STEPS CAN YOU TAKE BEFORE
YOU'RE GASPING FOR BREATH IN AN
ALARMING WAY _____

IDEAL DATE LOCATION: (THE _____
                BRANCH OF NANDO'S)

MAKE OF MOBILITY SCOOTER _____

WEEKS LEFT TO LIVE _____

DO ONE THING EVERY DAY THAT SGARES YOU!

THESE MAY INCLUDE:

GETTING A JOB
WASHING
EXPRESSING EMOTION
PAYING CHILD SUPPORT
BEING TOUCHED
VEGETABLES
LEAVING THE HOUSE
COLOURS
PEOPLE
ANIMALS
THINGS
ANYTHING UNDER 900 CALORIES
WEIRD SHAPED CLOUDS
WARMTH
YOUR OWN BREATHING
HAPPINESS

USE THIS PAGE TO GIVE
YOURSELF A PAPER CUT!

JUST SO YOU CAN ACTUALLY
FEEL SOMETHING FOR
ONCE IN YOUR LIFE.

[THIS PAGE HAS BEEN KEPT BLANK ON PURPOSE]

WRITE ABOUT HOW THAT MAKES YOU FEEL...

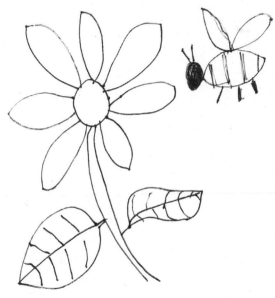

WRITE YOUR DEEPEST
DARKEST FANTASY ON
THIS PAGE. RIP IT OUT,
SCREW IT INTO A TINY BALL
AND DROP IT INTO THE
BICYCLE BASKET OF A
PASSING CLERGYMAN.
THAT'LL SHOW HIM.

HOW TO HAVE
IDEAS !

- BORROW THEM FROM SOMEONE SMARTER THAN YOU !

- TAKE THEM FROM THINGS YOU LIKE !

- PILFER THEM FROM SUCCESSFUL PEOPLE !

- RIP THEM OFF THE GREATS !

- COPY THEM OUT OF THINGS YOU HAVE LYING AROUND !

- STEAL THEM OFF THE INTERNET !

- HAVE FUN !

ON THIS PAGE, TELL ME THE LAST FIVE WEBSITES YOU VISITED!

1. _____ (OH WOW)

2. _____ (YEAH I'M BEGINNING TO REGRET THIS)

3. _____ (WHY ARE YOU TELLING ME THIS? HAVE YOU NO SHAME?)

4. _____ (THIS ONE WAS FEATURED IN THE TRIAL OF A PROMINENT 70s DJ)

5. _____ (GREAT. NOW I IMAGINE WE'RE BOTH ON SOME LIST)

IN THE SPACE BELOW, DESCRIBE
  YOURSELF WITHOUT USING THE
FOLLOWING WORDS:
SMALL! INSIGNIFICANT! PUMPKIN-LIKE!
GRIM! PETTY! HARD TO LIKE OR UNDERSTAND!
ROTTING! BROKEN! SWEATING! WEARS HATS!
SOMEWHAT EGGY! CRIES A LOT! FACILE!
ITCHY! A BIT RACIST! GRASPING! ASHY!
STAINED! REPELLENT! SCABBED! BLAND!
IN ARREARS! LOOKS LIKE THAT ONE OFF HOLBY!
ANAL! BANAL! CANAL OBSESSED! CAROL!
↓   ↓   ↓   ↓   ↓   ↓   ↓   ↓   ↓   ↓

TRICKY ISN'T IT?

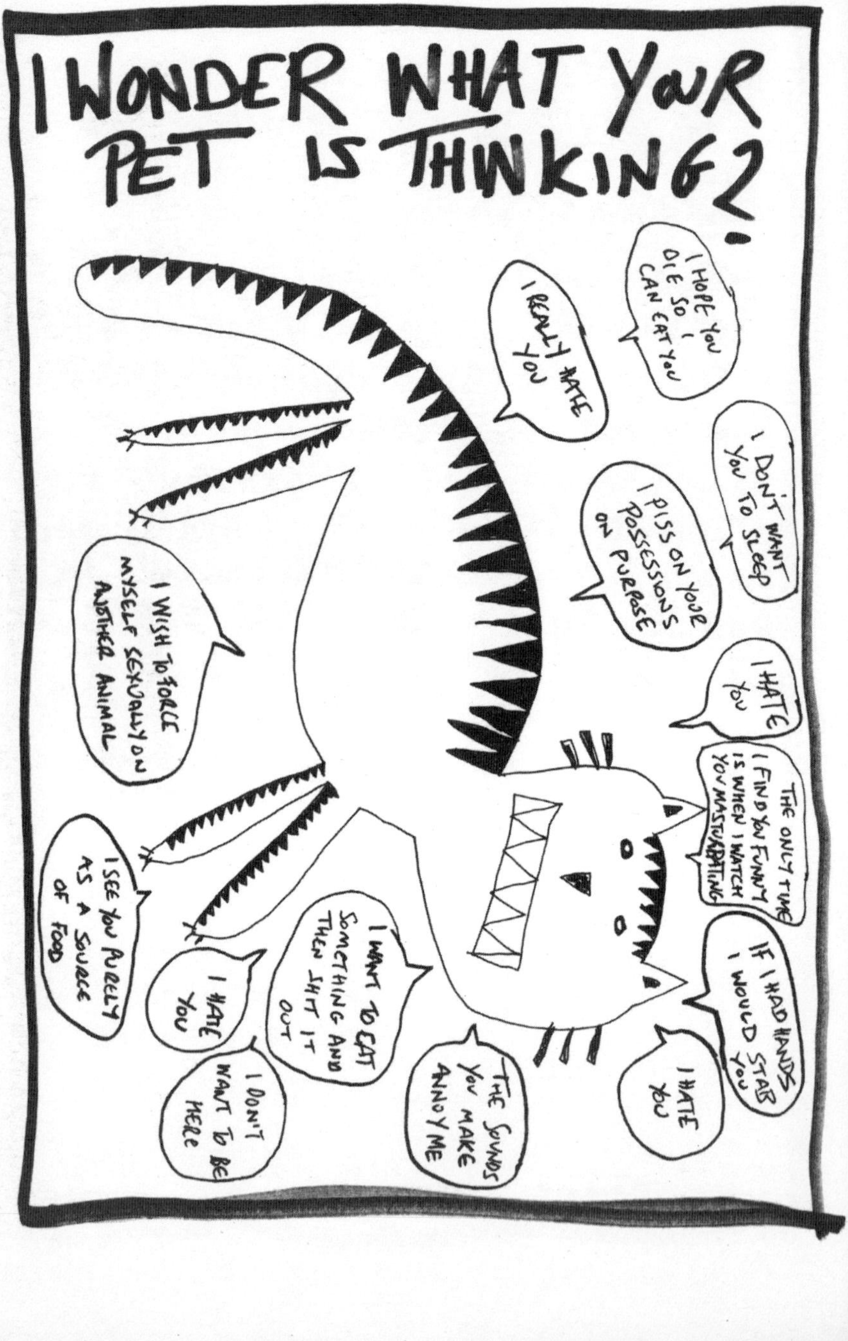
I WONDER WHAT YOUR PET IS THINKING?
I HOPE YOU DIE SO I CAN EAT YOU
I REALLY HATE YOU
I DON'T WANT YOU TO SLEEP
I PISS ON YOUR POSSESSIONS ON PURPOSE
I HATE YOU
THE ONLY TIME I FIND YOU FUNNY IS WHEN I WATCH YOU MASTURBATING
IF I HAD HANDS I WOULD STAB YOU
I HATE YOU
THE SOUNDS YOU MAKE ANNOY ME
I DON'T WANT TO BE HERE
I WANT TO EAT SOMETHING AND THEN SHIT IT OUT
I HATE YOU
I SEE YOU PURELY AS A SOURCE OF FOOD
I WISH TO FORCE MYSELF SEXUALLY ON ANOTHER ANIMAL

✳ OBVIOUSLY THIS DOESN'T APPLY IF YOU'RE MARRIED TO A PERSON LIKE MY EX-WIFE CAROL WHO ACTUALLY TOOK ALL THE CONDIMENTS WHEN SHE LEFT ME. TOOK. ALL. THE. CONDIMENTS. EVEN THE EXPIRED STUFF AND THINGS SHE DIDN'T LIKE. JUST LEFT ME SOME POPPADOMS. WHAT DOES THAT MEAN?

HERE'S A LIST OF INSPIRATIONAL WORDS TO FIND INSPIRING!

INSPIRE!
INSPIRATION!
INSPIRATIONAL!
INSPIRATIONALS!
INSPIRES!
AMAZING!
INSPIRED!
CREATE!
CREATIVE!
INSPIREDS!
THINKING!
THINK!
WORDS!
WINDOW!
IN-SPIRE!
THINKING!
DESPERATE!
DESPERATES!
INSPIRING!
DEADLINE!
FEAR!
FEAR!
CRIPPLING FEAR!
CREATE!
HUNGRY!
TEARS!
SCARED!
INSPIRE!
INSPIRED!
BOTTOM OF PAGE!

NEED A STORY?
LOOK OUT OF THE WINDOW!
SEE THAT PERSON OUT THERE?
THEY COULD BE A STORY!
WHAT'S THEIR NAME?
WHERE DO THEY GO?
FOLLOW THEM!
SEE WHERE THEY GO!
WHERE THEY EAT!
WHERE THEY LIVE!
HOW THEY MAKE LOVE!
ROOT THROUGH THEIR BINS!
TRAIN A TELEPHOTO LENS AT THEIR BEDROOM!
FIND OUT WHERE HER NEW HUSBAND WORKS!
SIT IN THE CAR PARK UNTIL HE LEAVES!
INTERCEPT THEIR MAIL!
ATTEND FAMILY EVENTS YOU WERE EXPRESSLY
                        FORBIDDEN FROM!
CREATE FAKE SOCIAL MEDIA PROFILES AND
                BEFRIEND HER CIRCLE!

CRY! CRY A LOT!

PLACE THIS PAGE IN A PUBLIC PLACE AND LET STRANGERS WRITE DOWN ALL YOUR OBVIOUS FAULTS!

↓ ↓ ↓ ↓ ↓ ↓ ↓ ↓ ↓

CHART YOUR PROGRESS ON THIS HANDY GRAPH!

FEIGNED INTEREST OF OTHERS

LEVEL OF POINTLESS EFFORT.

WHAT'S UNDER THE SHEET?

WRITE YOUR GUESS HERE

[CLUE: IT'S A POORLY ASSEMBLED AQUARIUM FILLED WITH A CONFUSING EASTERN EUROPEAN CORN-BASED SNACK BOUGHT IN BULK FROM A POUND SHOP]

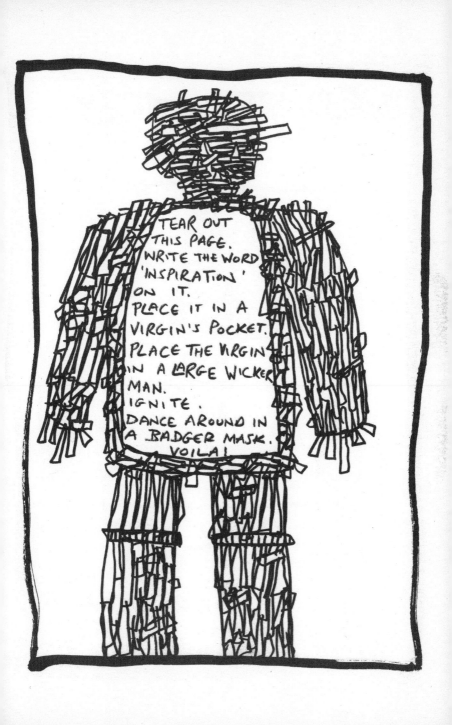

TEAR OUT
THIS PAGE.
WRITE THE WORD
'INSPIRATION'
ON IT.
PLACE IT IN A
VIRGIN'S POCKET.
PLACE THE VIRGIN
IN A LARGE WICKER
MAN.
IGNITE.
DANCE AROUND IN
A BADGER MASK.
VOILA!

SPOT THE

THEIR LIFE

[THERE ARE 12

DIFFERENCE!

YOUR LIFE

DIFFERENCES TO FIND!

I'VE WRITTEN A SONG FOR YOU!
JUST FILL IN THE BLANKS WITH YOUR NAME!

OH _____ YOU ARE A GREAT DISAPPOINTMENT TO ME.

YOU'RE ALMOST ILLEGALLY HAIRY _____

AND YOU SMELL OF PEE.

_____ YOU TURN MY STOMACH

AND HAVE NO ORIGINAL IDEAS

YOU APPAL ME _____

AND I'M ALMOST CERTAIN IT WAS YOU THAT STOLE MY CANESTEN

(CHORUS)

I HATE YOU I HATE YOU I HATE YOU

I HATE YOU I HATE YOU I HATE YOU

I HATE YOU I HATE YOU I HATE YOU

I REALLY HATE YOU _____

LISTEN!
CAN YOU HEAR THAT?
THAT'S THE SOUND OF YOUR INSPIR-
ATION

IT'S CALLING OUT TO YOU!

"LET ME OUT!" IT SAYS. "NO,
SERIOUSLY, LET ME OUT. I HAVE BEEN
TRAPPED HERE FOR A REALLY LONG TIME.
I CAN HELP AND INSPIRE YOU. LET ME OUT.
I HAVE NOT BEEN PROVIDED WITH ADEQUATE
FOOD AND WATER. THE SANITARY CONDITIONS
ARE HIDEOUS. I FREQUENTLY HAVE ELECTRODES
ATTACHED TO MY FEET AND GENITALS. I'M
BEATEN WITH TELEPHONE DIRECTORIES BY
MEN IN TRENCH COATS SEVERAL TIMES A
DAY. I HAVE TO SHIT IN A SAWN-OFF
TRAFFIC CONE. THERE IS ANOTHER MAN
HERE WHO HAS TAKEN ME FOR HIS
'INSIDE WIFE! PLEASE HELP ME BE
FREE." THAT IS YOUR INSPIRATION.

FILL THIS JAR WITH DRAWINGS OF DICKS!

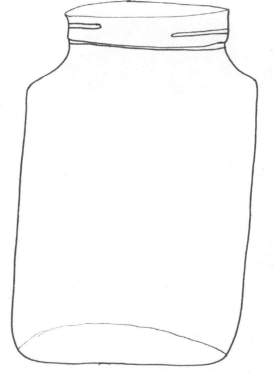

OR, IF YOU'RE A LADY, BOOBS!

NOW DROP THE BOOK IN A BIG MUDDY PUDDLE!

RIGHT. YOU DO REALISE YOU'VE NOW RUINED THE BOOK DON'T YOU? WHAT'S WRONG WITH YOU? DO YOU JUST BLINDLY DO ANYTHING THAT PEOPLE TELL YOU? BECAUSE THAT'S HOW NAZI GERMANY GOT STARTED. IS THAT WHAT YOU WANT?

HERE IS A BOX!

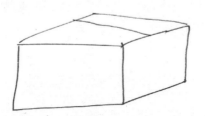

NOW THINK OUTSIDE IT!

HERE IS AN ENVELOPE!

NOW PUSH IT!
HERE IS SOME BULLSHIT!

NOW LAP IT UP!

OH DEAR! THIS POOR
DOGGIE'S WARMING
BLANKET NEEDS SOME
DECORATION...

WHY NOT MAKE IT LOOK
PRETTY BY WRITING YOUR
PIN NUMBER IN THERE!

[THEN FORWARD THE RESULTS, INCLUDING NAME
ADDRESS AND LOCATION DETAILS TO DALE SHAW,
% HEADLINE PUBLISHING, 50 VICTORIA EMBANKMENT,
LONDON, EC4Y 0DZ, UK]

THIS PAGE IS HOMEOPATHIC! JUST SNIFF IT WHEN YOU'RE SICK AND IT WILL FIX YOU! EVEN CANCER!

USE tHIS PAGE TO WRITE A RANSOM NOTE!

ADD PIECE OF VICTIM'S EAR HERE!

OH DEAR! SOMEONE'S MOVED TO YOUR NEIGHBOURHOOD WITH THE UNFORTUNATE NAME OF P.D. O'FILE! IT'S FAIR TO MAKE THE ASSUMPTION HE'S ON SOME SORT OF REGISTER, SO DAUB HIS FRONT DOOR WITH APPROPRIATE THREATS AND MESSAGES!
9

FREE PAGE!

THIS PAGE HAS BEEN PROVIDED FOR YOUR UNLIMITED USE! (THOUGH, OBVIOUSLY, I AM EMPTYING YOUR BANK ACCOUNT WHILE I HAVE YOU DISTRACTED.)

[THIS PAGE HAS BEEN KEPT BLANK ON PURPOSE]

WRITE ABOUT HOW THAT MAKES YOU FEEL...

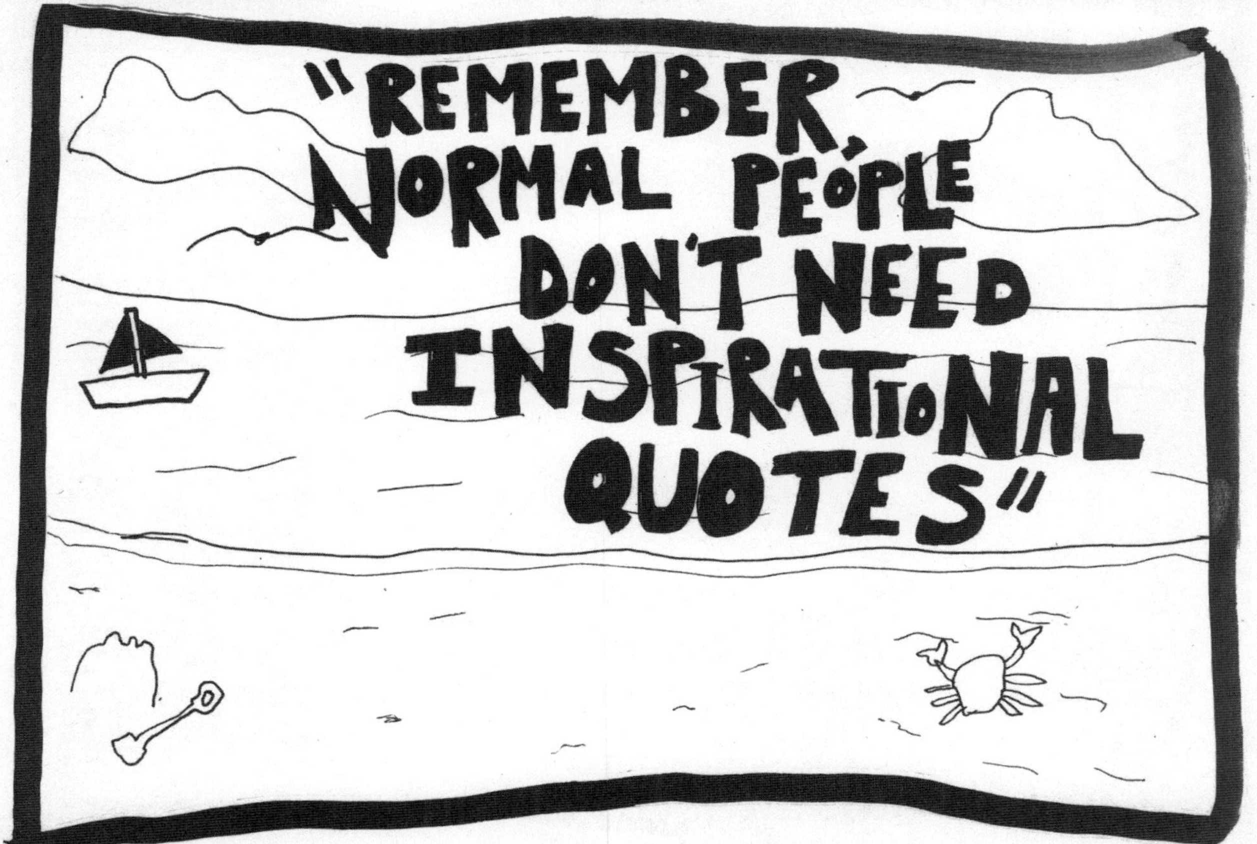
"REMEMBER, NORMAL PEOPLE DON'T NEED INSPIRATIONAL QUOTES"

TAPE THESE BARE

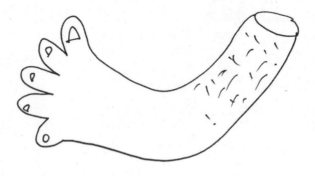

THEN SCUTTLE AROUND YOUR
MUMBLING ABOUT COVERT
WHILE CARRYING A FILTHY

PAGES TO YOUR FEET!

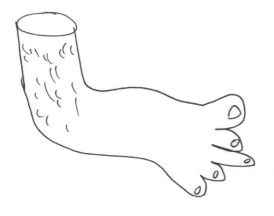

LOCAL SHOPPING PRECINCT, GOVERNMENT SURVEILLANCE TOTE BAG!

HERE'S YOUR CUT OUT
AND KEEP....
GLORY HOLE!

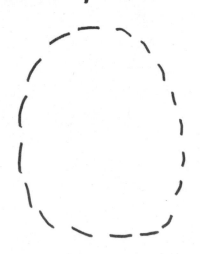

CLIP IT OUT FOR USE IN
PUBLIC BATHROOMS, PRIVATE
BATHROOMS OR BATHROOMS!
OH, AND GOOD LUCK!

DRAW A PICTURE OF YOUR FAVOURITE SHIRT AND POP IT IN THE WARDROBE!

IT WILL HELP YOU REMEMBER IT WHEN YOUR EX-WIFE DESTROYS ALL YOUR CLOTHES BY POURING BLEACH ON THEM AND THEN LEAVES YOU FOR A MAN WHO DOES CAR BOOT SALES FOR A LIVING. NO. HONESTLY. THAT'S ALL HE DOES. CAR BOOTS. TWO DAYS A WEEK. I GOT LEFT FOR THAT. SELLS LIKE SHAMPOO AND SPONGES

TEAR OUT THIS
PAGE - BALL IT UP
AND HURL IT AT
THE OLDEST OR
WEAKEST MEMBER
OF YOUR FAMILY!
YOU KNOW- FOR FUN!

EXCELLENT! YOUR MATE SPAIGE GOT DRUNK AND PASSED OUT ON A CROSS CHANNEL FERRY! IT IS YOUR DUTY TO SCRAWL COCKS ON HIS FACE, SHAVE OFF HIS EYEBROWS AND WRITE INSULTING MESSAGES!

GO WILD!

FILL THIS PAGE WITH LOTS OF CRAZY SCRIBBLES! LIKE THIS!

WOW! THAT WAS REALLY FUN!

OH NO! LOOK OUT! IT'S DOG SHIT!
(NO, NOT THIS. I WAS TALKING ABOUT YOUR LIFE. THIS IS HUMAN SHIT.)

BE THE STAR OF YOUR OWN
MOVIE!

HERE ARE SOME TITLES TO AVOID:

THE CHILD STRANGLER

RABBIT PROOF FENCE II

I PORK HUCKABEES

THE TOPLESSEST BANK HEIST IN THE WHOLE WIDE WORLD.

BREAKFAST WITH A MASTURBATOR

THE CHILLENING

KRULL BUT NUDE.

SMELLS AND TASTES LIKE SHIT.

IT'S NOT SEXUAL (IT'S ALWAYS SEXUAL)

I'LL WEAR YOU LIKE A FANCY HAT

HOPE SPONGE

THE NUN SHOVELER

ANYTHING WITH ZACH BRAFF

BLOOD ON THE TOILET PAPER

THE WHALES OF AUGUST

SPANKED ALONE.

JUST RUB IT IN BRISKLY

COLD, DISTANT AND ALWAYS SCREAMING

YOU CAN'T SPELL ADULTERY WITHOUT [INSERT NAME HERE]

I AM A WRITER AND Jo CAN YOU BE TOO!

" I THOUGHT SUCHET WAS THE ONLY DECENT POIROT. PISSED ALL OVER THE REST OF THEM. I MEAN, ALBERT FINNEY? HE'S BUILT LIKE A DOCKER. BIG LEGS. I LOOK MORE BELGIAN THAN HIM. AND BLOODY USTINOV? CHRIST. HE WAS ALL OVER THE SHOP. YOU CAN'T JUST SLAP A MOUSTACHE ON A FAT BLOKE AND GET THEM TO TALK LIKE PEPE LE PEW. FUCKING RIDICULOUS. "

AGATHA "MARPLE" CHRISTIE.

FREE PAGE!

YOU CAN USE THIS PAGE TO DO ANYTHING YOU WANT!

Though, sadly, I have decided to fill most of it with a picture of some jeggings.

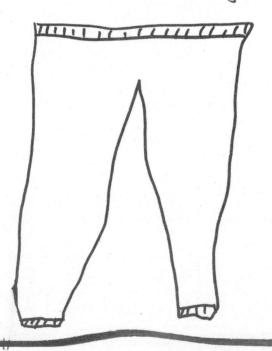

REMEMBER!

IF ALL ELSE FAILS

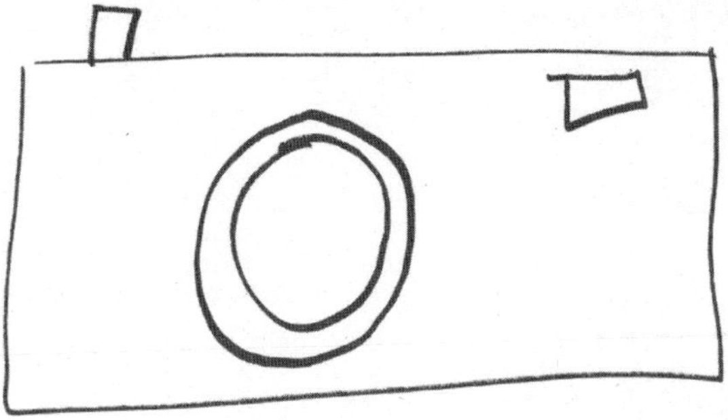

YOU CAN ALWAYS BE A

PHOTOGRAPHER!

TURN THE PAGE USING
THE LEAST HORRIFYING
PART OF YOUR BODY!

[IT'S OK - TAKE AS LONG AS YOU NEED TO MAKE YOUR
CHOICE]

ADVICE TO IGNORE!

" TAKE IT ONE DAY AT A TIME! "

(TERRIBLE. YOU HAVE NO CHOICE)

" THE GRASS IS ALWAYS GREENER..! "

(THE ONLY BIT OF GRASS I CAN SEE IS SOME WASTE GROUND COVERED IN OLD FRIDGES AND DOG SHIT)

" DO UNTO OTHERS AS YOU WOULD HAVE DONE TO YOU! "

(NO DON'T. I'M A SHIT TO MOST PEOPLE BUT IF THEY GIVE ME LIP, I KICK OFF)

" THERE'S PLENTY MORE FISH IN THE SEA! "

(NOT IF I'VE GOT ANYTHING TO DO WITH IT)

" WHERE THERE'S LIFE, THERE'S HOPE! "

(I COULDN'T DISAGREE MORE)

" CHEER UP! IT MIGHT NEVER HAPPEN! "

(IT WILL AND HAS)

" NEVER MASTURBATE ON PUBLIC TRANSPORT! "

(THAT SOUNDS LIKE A CHALLENGE TO ME!)

I WROTE THIS PAGE WITH THE LIGHTS OFF!

YOU TRY IT TOO!

[AND REMEMBER, DARKNESS IS YOUR FRIEND]

DRAW SOME
OVERLY BUSHY
EYEBROWS ON THE
POTENTIAL PAEDOPHILE!

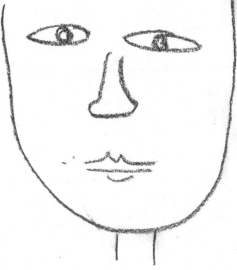

(AND MAYBE A SCRAGGLY CRUMB-FILLED
BEARD JUST TO BE ON THE SAFE SIDE)

CAREFULLY
REMOVE
THIS
PAGE FROM
THE
BOOK !

THIS
ONE
Too!

AND
ME!

THEN THIS
FINAL ONE!.
LAY THEM OUT END
TO END.
THAT'S THE EXACT DISTANCE
YOU'RE LEGALLY OBLIGED
TO STAY AWAY FROM THE
PROPERTY OF YOUR EX-WIFE
CAROL! ISN'T THAT FUN?.
THANK YOU JUSTICE
EDWARD FRITH AND
EVERYONE AT THE LAW
FIRM OF HAYES, CREST
AND GREENOBLE!.
KEEP UP THE GOOD
WORK!

MISERY = MOOLAH!

DID YOU HAVE A TERRIBLE, DAMAGING CHILDHOOD? GREAT!
WRITE IT UP AS A MISERY MEMOIR!
FILL IN THE BLANKS AND FEEL FREE TO USE THESE TITLES!

"DADDY SLAMMED MY ____ IN THE ____ FOR ____ YEARS"

"____ LOCKED ME IN THE ____ FREEZER"

"____ AND THE ____ UP THE ____"

"____ WASN'T MY GRANDPA HE WAS MY ____"

"SCUTTLED BY ____"

"MY STEP-____ MADE ME EAT ____"

"NOW I HAVE ____ FOR ARMS"

"____ ____ LABRADOR ____"

TAKE TWO BOOKS!
STICK THEM UP THE SLEEVES OF YOUR JACKET!

THEN PRETEND TO BE BILLY BOOK HANDS!!

[THAT SHOULD KILL A COUPLE OF MINUTES]

WANT TO BE AN ARTIST?

DON'T FORGET THE MOST IMPORTANT THING!

TROUSERS!

ALWAYS ENSURE YOUR TROUSERS ARE BAFFLING AND EXTREME.

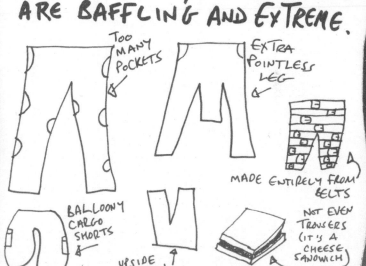

TOO MANY POCKETS

EXTRA POINTLESS LEG

MADE ENTIRELY FROM BELTS

BALLOONY CARGO SHORTS

UPSIDE DOWN

NOT EVEN TROUSERS (IT'S A CHEESE SANDWICH)

LET'S PLAY SWEAR TRAIN!

I'M GOING TO WRITE A SWEAR. THE NEXT PERSON HAS TO WRITE THE NEXT SWEAR USING THE LAST LETTER OF THE PREVIOUS SWEAR.. IF YOU CAN'T THINK OF ONE; MAKE IT UP!

TITWRINGER RECTUM _____

INSPO TIP!

DON'T FALL FOUL OF VALIDATION VAMPIRES! THE FOLLOWING GROUPS OF PEOPLE WILL CLOG YOUR CREATIVITY, SO AVOID AT ALL COSTS!

FRIENDS	LOVED ONES	CRONIES
FAMILY	NEIGHBOURS	WELL-WISHERS
CHUMS	STRANGERS	PARENTS
PALS	FELLOWS	SIDEKICKS
TEACHERS	BUDDIES	COMPADRES
RELATIVES	INTIMATES	GURUS
MATES	RELATIONS	MENTORS
ACQUAINTANCES	KIN	ACCOMPLICES
CO-WORKERS	OFFSPRING	ABETTORS
ASSOCIATES	PARTNERS	POLICEMEN
COLLEAGUES	ALLIES	FLUNKIES
PALSIE-WALSIES	CONFIDANTS	JUNKIES
SPOUSES	SUPPORTERS	HUNKS
COMPANIONS	CELL MATES	UNCLES
	MUCKERS	ENEMIES
	PETS	PEOPLE

WHAT ARE YOUR TOP FIVE FAVE MOVIES?

1. _____ (WRONG)

2. _____ (TERRIBLE)

3. _____ (RIGHT, So You ARE ACTUALLY 9 YEARS OLD)

4. _____ (YOU'VE NEVER SEEN THAT. AND IF YOU HAVE THERE'S NO WAY YOU UNDERSTOOD IT. I HAD TO EXPLAIN RATATOUILLE TO YOU. JUST ADMIT IT. YOU'RE NOT THAT SMART. IT'S NOTHING TO BE ASHAMED OF).

5. _____ (No.)

You ARE A
STAR!

DIM, DISTANT AND
DEAD INSIDE.

HERE'S A PAIR OF EYES!
WHY NOT DRAW A FUNNY FACE
AROUND IT!

WAIT. IS THAT SUPPOSED TO BE ME? NO, I'M SORRY
IT LOOKS JUST LIKE ME. YOU'VE GOT MY SCAR
IN THE SHAPE OF A HARPSICHORD AND EVERYTHING. YES
IT IS! NO ONE ELSE HAS THAT HAIRLINE. AND MY
DISTINCTIVE CHEEK PIERCING? IT'S TOO MUCH OF A
COINCIDENCE. IS THAT HOW YOU SEE ME? OR ARE YOU
JUST DESPERATE TO HURT ME? WHY? THAT'S ALL I
WANT TO KNOW. WHY??

USE THIS PAGE TO WRAP UP
THIS BOOK WHEN YOU
INEVITABLY REGIFT IT
AS YOU DON'T REALLY GET
IT. AND YOUR COUSIN WITH
THE FUNNY EYE HAS A
DAMGAGED SENSE OF HUMOUR
AND WILL PROBABLY APPRECIATE IT.

MAKE THE WHOLE WORLD YOUR CANVAS!

SCRAWL "INSPIRATION!" ON EVERY WALL YOU SEE!

SPRAY-PAINT "CREATIVITY!" AGAINST EVERY AVAILABLE SURFACE!

PISS "IDEAS!" ON A TREE IN A MEMORIAL PARK!

CARVE "ARTFULNESS!" ONTO AN ORNAMENTAL SUN-DIAL DEDICATED TO FALLEN SAILORS!

STAB "WONDER!" INTO A PIG CARCASS!

SPANK "ENERGY!" ONTO THE TENDER BARE BUTTOCKS OF A MALAY!

COLOUR ME IN!
[DIGNITY IS OVER-RATED!]
"FORMER DOCTOR WHO COLIN BAKER SENDING BACK A CROISSANDWICH BECAUSE IT HAD EGG ON IT."

FIND YOUR INSPIRATION NAME!

TAKE YOUR MOST INSULTING NICKNAME FROM SCHOOL!

THEN ADD YOUR LEAST SATISFYING SEXUAL PARTNER!

PUT THEM TOGETHER AND VOILA! INSPIRATION NAME!

[MINE IS "PISSFINGERS LUSARDI"]

FREE PAGE!

THIS IS A FREE PAGE WHERE YOU CAN DO WHATEVER YOU WISH!

[I KNOW IT'S NOT EXACTLY 'FREE', AS YOU PAID FOR THE BOOK IN THE FIRST PLACE. OR, MORE LIKELY, RECEIVED IT AS A LAST MINUTE, DESPERATE, SECRET SANTA AFTERTHOUGHT FROM A CO-WORKER WHO MISTAKENLY CALLS YOU 'MIKE' AND WHO YOU THINK MIGHT BE BEHIND ALL THOSE 'HAD SEX WITH A SCHNAUZER' RUMOURS.]

TIME TO JOIN THE DOTS FUN!

HOW TO BE A YOU TUBE SUPERSTAR!

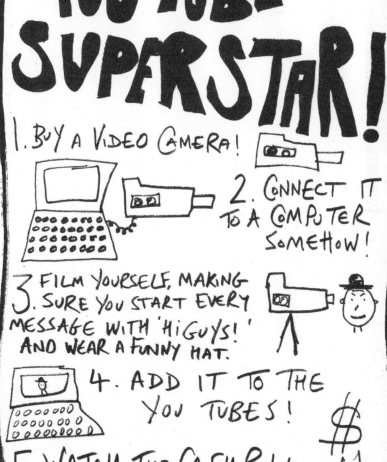

1. BUY A VIDEO CAMERA!

2. CONNECT IT TO A COMPUTER SOMEHOW!

3. FILM YOURSELF, MAKING SURE YOU START EVERY MESSAGE WITH 'HI GUYS!' AND WEAR A FUNNY HAT.

4. ADD IT TO THE YOU TUBES!

5. WATCH THE CASH ROLL IN!

DISASTER! THIS PAINFULLY STYLISH HIPSTER HAS LEFT THE HOUSE WITHOUT HIS TRADEMARK FACIAL HAIR, TERRIBLE PIERCINGS, IRONIC TATTOOS AND CLOTHES THAT MAKE YOU GAG! SO DRAW THEM ON! (DON'T FORGET THE BRACES!)

THIS PAGE IS
UPSIDE DOWN!
[IT WASN'T SUPPOSED TO BE.
BUT THAT'S WHAT YOU GET
WHEN YOU SEND YOUR
STUFF OVERSEAS TO BE
PRINTED. CHEAP BUT
UNRELIABLE.]

START AN ARGUMENT!

HERE ARE SOME HELPFUL OPENING GAMBITS:

"WHY IS YOUR FACE LIKE THAT?"

"I JUST PISSED ALL OVER THOSE..."

"YOU'RE JUST LIKE YOUR MOTHER. A POINTLESS LITTLE BITCH."

"I FIND YOUR OPINIONS CUTE."

"IS THE FAT BLOKE FROM LOST YOUR DAD OR SOMETHING?"

"THERE'S SOMETHING ABOUT YOU THAT MAKES ME WANT TO COMPETELY GIVE UP HOPE."

"SO... RECTAL HYGIENE NEVER MEANT THAT MUCH TO YOU?"

"GOOD CHRIST YOU'RE A CHUNKY ONE."

"PUKE WOULD IMPROVE YOU."

"IN CONCLUSION: BALL SACK."

"GO FULK YOURSELF."

DRAW YOUR FAVOURITE PLACE TO HIDE AND CRY!

[MINE IS A COSTA COFFEE IN BRENT CROSS SHOPPING CENTRE]

INSPIRATION IS NOT A ONE-WAY STREET!

No, IT'S A ONE-WAY STREET WITH A BIKE MESSENGER BARRELLING TOWARDS YOU RIDING THE WRONG WAY AND HE'S WHITE AND HE HAS DREADLOCKS AND SWEARS AT YOU AS HE PASSES.

HOLD THIS PAGE UP TO THE
LIGHT! CAN YOU SEE A
WATERMARK OFFERING AN
INSPIRATIONAL MESSAGE?
IF YOU CAN'T, IT MEANS WE
COULDN'T AFFORD THE
MANUFACTURING PROCESS
REQUIRED TO DO THIS.
WRITE ABOUT HOW THAT
MAKES YOU FEEL.

DRUGS!!

SOME OF YOUR FAVOURITE INSPIRATIONAL FIGURES HAVE HAD THEIR MOST CREATIVE MOMENTS ON DRUGS. SO WHY NOT GIVE IT A GO!

JUST WALK UP TO A SEEDY LOOKING MAN AND ASK FOR THE FOLLOWING: NEBS, SUDGE, CLACKERS, BAD ANTHRACITE, KHX, LEONARD, STICKLEBRICKS, PAMPT, WET LEMON, TESSA SANDERSON, BLUK, NANO GLITTER, THE SHEM, MICKLEMAS, GANGLE, BOOOOOOO BS, DRUGS 2·0, POODGE, MANNED FAT.

BE LIKE A BANKSY! SPRAY PAINT SOME-THING ON THIS WALL!

[LIKE, Y'KNOW, THE QUEEN SMOKING A DOOBIE OR THE POPE ON THE PHONE. SOMETHING LIKE THAT.]

WHISPER IN MY EAR AND
TELL ME THE NAME OF
     YOUR BEST FRIEND...

WRITE NAME HERE:

[WARNING: YOU CANNOT PICK WIVES,
EX-WIVES, GIRLFRIENDS OR
SIGNIFICANT OTHERS. THEY MAY
ACT LIKE A FRIEND BUT ALL THAT
CHANGES WHEN YOU GET TO COURT.
SOME OF THE THINGS SHE SAID
ABOUT ME. IT WAS UNBELIEVABLE.
'BORDERLINE PSYCHOTIC.' YEAH THAT'S
REALLY FUCKING FRIENDLY. TWELVE
YEARS AND THAT'S WHAT YOU END
UP WITH. IT'S A FUCKING JOKE.]

ON A BUS? SING A SONG ABOUT THE PERSON SITTING NEXT TO YOU? IF THEY LOOK UPSET – SING LOUDER! IF THEY BEGIN TO CRY – ADD THAT TO THE LYRICS! IF THEY GET OFF – FOLLOW THEM SINGING EVEN LOUDER AND MOCKING THE WAY THAT THEY WALK!

WRITE ABOUT HOW THAT MAKES YOU FEEL.

CUT TWO EYE-HOLES IN THIS PAGE.
NOW YOU CAN ACT LIKE A SPY!

[JUST DON'T DO IT AT THE GYMN OR NEAR
THE SWIMMING POOL CHANGING ROOMS AS
"APPARENTLY" THAT'S CONSIDERED "BEHAVIOUR
LIKELY TO CAUSE OFFENCE" WHICH WOULD
RESULT IN "IMMEDIATE EXPULSION AND
POSSIBLE CRIMINAL PROCEEDINGS." Dicks.]

I AM A WRITER AND SO CAN YOU BE TOO!
"LOOK, I DON'T KNOW WHERE THESE RUMOURS STARTED. ALL I KNOW IS, IF IT HAD A PAIR OF TITS, I'D PROBABLY HAVE A CRACK AT IT."
OSCAR 'A HANDBAG' WILDE.

DRAW THE VIOLENT
DISEMBOWLING OF
THE ASSHOLE WHO GOT
YOU THIS STUPID BOOK!
↓ ↓ ↓ ↓ ↓ ↓ ↓

[THIS PAGE HAS BEEN KEPT BLANK ON PURPOSE]

WRITE ABOUT HOW THAT MAKES YOU FEEL...

WRITE YOUR NAME HERE!

_____

NOW WRITE A FUNNY NAME!

_____

OH RIGHT, IS THAT WHAT YOU'RE GOING WITH?

No, No. IT'S 'FINE'! MORE PITHY THAN FUNNY

I JUST USE AIR-QUOTES SOMETIMES, IT DOESN'T MEAN ANYTHING.

I'M NOT PASSIVE-AGGRESSIVE. YOU CAN'T TAKE CRITICISM.

YOU CAN'T!

No, YOU CAN'T!

OK, LET'S NOT SAY THINGS WE CAN'T TAKE BACK.

WOW. JUST WOW. ARE YOU PROUD OF YOURSELF? USING LANGUAGE LIKE THAT?

MY MOTHER IS A SAINT!

TELL YOU WHAT. YOU WRITE WHERE YOU CAN GO FUCK YOURSELF

_____

DECORATE THIS PAGE WITH THE BLOOD OF A FARM ANIMAL!*

*DON'T ASK THE FARMER'S PERMISSION. HE'LL SAY NO.

I AM A WRITER AND SO CAN YOU BE TOO!

"I'VE TOLD THEM KIDS OVER AND OVER THAT THE GARAGE ROOF WON'T TAKE THEIR WEIGHT AND THEY'LL GO RIGHT THROUGH IT IF THEY KEEP TITTING ABOUT UP THERE. BUT THEY WON'T LISTEN. I CAN SEE THEM UP THERE NOW. LITTLE SHITS."

EMILE "THE ONE THAT ISN'T BALZAC" ZOLA.

INSPIRATION DO'S AND DON'TS! ...

DO: HAVE GREAT IDEAS!

DON'T: SMELL SOMEONE'S HAIR AS THEY SLEEP.

DO: BE POSITIVE!

DON'T: EAT STUFF YOU FIND DOWN A WELL.

DO: THINK CREATIVELY!

DON'T: NAME ANY OF YOUR CHILDREN 'CUDGEL' OR 'CLAMMY'.

DO: EMBRACE MINDFULNESS!

DON'T: BELIEVE ANYTHING A CARTOON CAT TELLS YOU.

DO: EXUDE ENERGY!

DON'T: TRY TO BE 'FUNNY' WITH THE BAILIFFS.

DO: CONTINUE BEING AWESOME!

DON'T: DRUNKENLY CALL YOUR EX-WIFE FROM THE BOOKIES AND START CRYING.

IN THIS SPACE, LEAVE YOUR THUMB PRINT!

←

IN THIS BOX WRITE YOUR FULL LEGAL NAME!

→

THEN IN THE AREA BELOW SIGN OVER POWER OF ATTORNEY TO ME! AND POP IT IN THE POST!

I, THE UNDERSIGNED, HEREBY DECLARE THAT THE FOLLOWING INDIVIDUAL MR. DALE SHAW HAS LASTING POWER OF ATTORNEY REGARDING ANY FINANCIAL AFFAIRS CONNECTED TO MY ESTATE, IN PERPETUITY AND FOR EVER MORE.

_____   _____   _____
(SIGNED)   (DATE)   (WITNESS)

YOU'RE RIGHT IN THE MIDDLE OF THE BOOK!

NOW YOU CAN WEAR IT LIKE A HAT!*

* Warning – do not use this book as a hat in electrical storms or high wind areas. Never use the book as a hat in any construction settings or during competitive sporting events. Never use the book as a makeshift helmet when mining or riding a scooter or Segway or horse. The book, when used as a hat, will become damaged in times of high precipitation. The publishers of this book prohibit its use from entry into a regional Easter bonnet competition or 'who has the best hat' event at a local fete or Springtime Dance function. Using the hat to perform racist imitations of South Sea Islanders or the Irish voids its warranty. Purchasers wear the book as a hat at their own risk. The author or publisher are not liable for any paper cuts, chafing or neck injuries suffered if the book is worn as a hat. Do not use the book as a hat in any medical or aquatic situations. Not to be used as a hat outside the EU.

TO CELEBRATE YOUR

AWESOMENESS

HERE'S A FIREWORKS
DISPLAY!

OH YEAH, YOU CAN'T REALLY SEE
ANYTHING DUE TO FOG AND, LIKE ALL
FIREWORKS DISPLAYS, IT WOULD HAVE
BEEN DISAPPOINTING ANYWAY AND
THE FIREWORKS DISPLAY WAS
CANCELLED. HAPPY BIRTHDAY.

JUST SCAN THE QR
CODE FOR ADDITIONAL
    CONTENT!

IF IT DOESN'T WORK,
DON'T WORRY!
JUST BUY ANOTHER
    BOOK!

FREE PAGE!

THINK OF IT AS A WIDE OPEN PASTURE WAITING FOR YOU TO SKIP AND GAMBOL, TOSSING INSPIRATIONAL IDEAS INTO THE AIR LIKE DELICIOUS POSIES! THOUGH WATCH OUT FOR THE FARMER! HE'S HIGH ON METH AND BRANDISHING A METAL POLE.

IN THE BOX BELOW
TELL ME YOUR
FAVOURITE WORD!

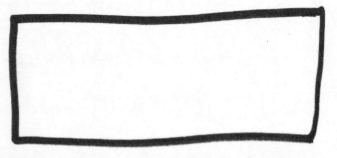

WOW. ERM, MAYBE IT'S A
GENERATIONAL THING BUT
THAT'S NOT REALLY A WORD
THAT GETS USED IN POLITE
COMPANY ANYMORE. AND
THAT'S YOUR FAVOURITE?
REALLY? THAT'S PRETTY CREEPY.

REMEMBER, THERE'S NO SUCH
THING AS A BAD IDEA!
OH, EXCEPT FOR THAT ONE
YOU HAD ABOUT QUITTING YOUR
JOB AND GOING BACK TO COLLEGE
TO TRAIN AS A NAIL TECHNICIAN.
I MEAN, WHAT WERE YOU THINKING? I
COULDN'T SUPPORT US BOTH ON WHAT I
MAKE. YOU THINK THIS THING IS GOING
TO COVER US? THIS BOOK? THIS THING
IS GOING TO DRAG US BOTH DOWN TO
OBLIVION. WE'LL PROBABLY BOTH BE
TAKING SECOND JOBS AFTER THIS
DEBACLE. OH AND THE ONE YOU HAD
ABOUT TIES FOR DOGS. THAT WAS A
BAD IDEA TOO.

DESIGN THE COVER OF YOUR SOLO ALBUM!

I'LL PROVIDE THE AMAZON REVIEWS:

⭐⭐☆☆ "ONE STAR. PAINFUL AND UNFORTUNATE."

⭐☆☆☆☆ "ONE STAR. INEXPLICABLE USE OF A ZITHER"

⭐☆☆☆☆ "ONE STAR. THE SOUNDTRACK TO MEDIOCRITY."

⭐☆☆☆☆ "ONE STAR. A MASH-UP OF GASSY BEATS + SCABS"

⭐☆☆☆☆ "ONE STAR. LIKE CHEEKY GIRLS + VENGA BOYS HAD A BABY."

⭐☆☆☆☆ "ONE STAR. PITIFUL"

⭐☆☆☆☆ "ONE STAR. THE MUSICAL EQUIVALENT OF AN STD."

TELL ME YOUR FIRST EVER...

PET MURDER _____

EROTIC ENCOUNTER
INVOLVING SOMEONE
WEARING BICYCLE SHORTS _____

EJECTION FROM A SNAPPY SNAPS _____

DRUG BUST _____

ANAL BLEACHING GONE AWRY _____

TIME YOU WERE DESCRIBED
AS 'DUMPY' _____

ORAL GRATIFICATION OF A
ZOO KEEPER _____

WEEPING FOR NO
REASON _____

INFORMATION + INSPIRATION = INSPIRMATION!

IT MUST BE GOOD! IT SOUNDS LIKE IT'S GOT "SPERM"

RIGHT IN THE MIDDLE OF IT!

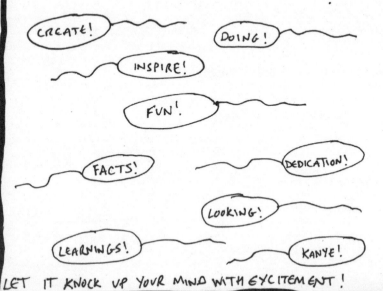

LET IT KNOCK UP YOUR MIND WITH EXCITEMENT!

A. Q. E. E.

"ALWAYS QUESTION EVERYTHING EVER"

THE CREATIVE MIND IS INQUISITIVE.

SO ASK QUESTIONS LIKE THESE:

"WHAT'S INSIDE THAT AMBULANCE?"

"HOW IS THERE GOTHS?"

"IS THIS THE RIGHT ROAD FOR UTOXETER?"

"YOU LOOK LIKE HAROLD SHIPMAN?"

"DID YOU PACK THOSE SWEATPANTS YOURSELF?"

"WHY IS THIS ALL SO GREASY?"

"ARE YOU SURE IT CAN BE EATEN LIKE THAT?"

"WHERE DID YOU FIND THESE BOZOS?"

"EVEN THE CARPET? WOW."

"COULD YOU LIFT UP THE ARM REST? IT'S CHAFING."

LOOK AT THAT!
A BIRD HAS
POOPED ON THIS
PAGE!
THAT'S GOOD LUCK!
CONGRATS!

[JUST MAKE SURE IT IS ACTUALLY
BIRD POOP AND NOT THAT WEIRD
BLOKE WHO LIVES IN THE FLAT
UPSTAIRS AND SHITS OFF THE
BALCONY. THAT IS NO LONGER
CONSIDERED LUCKY.]

WRITE YOUR SUPERHERO NAME ON THE BACK OF THIS CAPE!

[TIP: TRY TO UTILISE YOUR STRONGEST CHARACTER TRAITS I.E. "CRYINGMAN", "ODOURGIRL" OR "THE MASKED PRICK"

MAKE YOUR OWN RUBIK'S CUBE!

FIRST! COLOUR THESE SQUARES IN THE SAME COLOURS AS A RUBIK'S CUBE:

NOW! CAREFULLY CUT THEM OUT WITH SCISSORS.

THEN! GET A RUBIK'S CUBE AND PEEL OFF ALL THE SQUARES.

FINALLY! STICK ON YOUR NEW SQUARES. VOILA! YOUR OWN RUBIK'S CUBE!

HURRAH! YOU HAVE RETURNED HOME TO DISCOVER A RAVING DERELICT ON YOUR DOORSTEP! WRITE DOWN ALL THE CRAZY THINGS HE SAYS!

DRAW CLUSTERS OF PAINFUL SICKENING ACNE ON THE FACE OF THIS TEEN FAST FOOD WORKER!

RUN OUTSIDE!
FIND A FEATHER!
STICK IT TO THIS PAGE!
NOW WASH YOUR HANDS!
NO, I MEAN REALLY
    WASH THEM!
MAKE THE WATER AS HOT AS
    YOU CAN STAND!
AND USE SOME ANTI-BACTERIAL
    SANITISER.
LOOK, IT WAS PROBABLY A PIGEON
    FEATHER.
DO YOU KNOW HOW FILTHY THOSE THINGS
    ARE?
THEY ARE CRAWLING WITH LICE. AND A DOG
    PROBABLY DID A SHIT ON IT.
AND NOT A NICE DOG.
IF YOU TOUCHED YOUR EYES OR MOUTH
    AFTER TOUCHING THE FEATHER - RUSH
TO THE NEAREST MEDICAL FACILITY.
    YOU MAY ALREADY HAVE PSITTACOSIS.
I WILL PRAY FOR YOU.
    ALL THAT IS LEFT IS PRAYER!

HAVE AN ADVENTURE!

JUMP ON THE FIRST BUS YOU SEE!

TELL THE DRIVER: "I'M HAVING AN ADVENTURE!"

TAKE A SEAT! WHEN THE DRIVER DEMANDS YOU PAY, SAY: "I'M HAVING AN ADVENTURE!"

WHEN THE OTHER PASSENGERS START SHOUTING, TELL THEM: "I'M HAVING AN ADVENTURE!"

WHEN THE POLICE ARE CALLED, SCREAM: "I'M HAVING AN ADVENTURE! I'M HAVING AN ADVENTURE! I'M HAVING A FUCKING ADVENTURE!"

VIVE LA DIFFÉRENCE!

☆   ☆

BEING DIFFERENT IS GREAT!
WHY NOT RUN OUTSIDE AND FIND
        SOMEONE WHO LOOKS DIFFERENT!
THEN STARE AT THEM TO REALLY
    GET A FEEL FOR DIFFERENCES!
POINT OUT THEIR DIFFERENCES IN
            A LOUD VOICE!
THEN IN THE SPACE BELOW, DRAW
    THEIR DIFFERENCES. THEN GIVE
        THEM THE PICTURE AS A NICE GIFT!
    ↓   ↓   ↓   ↓   ↓   ↓   ↓

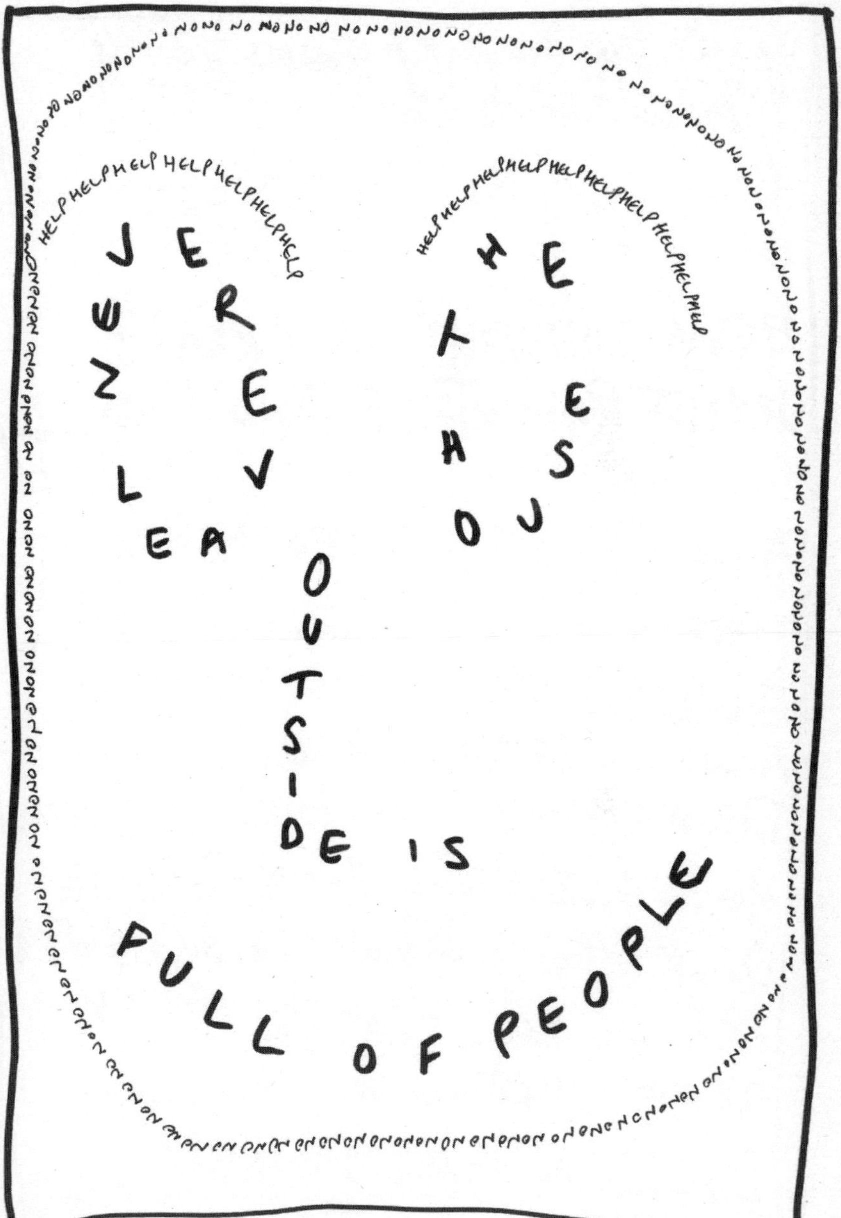

NO NO NO NO NO NO NO NO NO NO NO NO NO NO NO NO NO NO NO

HELP HELP HELP HELP HELP HELP HELP   HELP HELP HELP HELP HELP HELP HELP HELP

NEVER LEAVE   THE HOUSE

OUTSIDE IS

FULL OF PEOPLE

FIND AN INSPIRATIONAL THING!
LOOK CREATIVE!
OPEN YOUR MIND TO MINDFULNESS!
GO FOR IT!
GO FOR IT AGAIN!
INSERT EXCLAMATION POINTS!
NEVER NOT BE CREATIVE!
GO FOR IT!

ADD INSPIRATIONAL ELEMENTS!

DON'T BE UNINSPIRED!
EXIST CREATIVELY!
ALWAYS BE INSPIRED!
DRINK RESPONSIBLY!

HAVE CREATIVE THOUGHTS!
OPERATE INSPIRATIONALLY!
REALLY BE CREATIVE!
STUFF INSPIRATION INTO EVERY ORIFICE!
EXCEL IN EVERYTHING!

THIS
PAGE
IS BLACK
(LIKE THE
DEEPEST
RECESSES
OF YOUR
SOUL)

IN THE SPACE BELOW
DRAW A BRILLIANT PONY!
[ACTUALLY JUST LOOK AT
THIS DRAWING OF A PONY]

YOU WERE NEVER ANY GOOD
AT DRAWING PONIES.

IT'S CHOOSE YOUR OWN ADVENTURE TIME!

YOU ARE A WARRIOR.
YOU ENTER A CAVE.
AHEAD OF YOU ARE TWO TUNNELS.
ONE HAS A FAINT GLOW.
THE OTHER HAS YOUR EX-WIFE CAROL IN IT.

TO TAKE THE GLOWING TUNNEL TURN TO
THE NEXT PAGE

TO TAKE THE CAROL TUNNEL TURN TO
THE PAGE AFTER THAT...

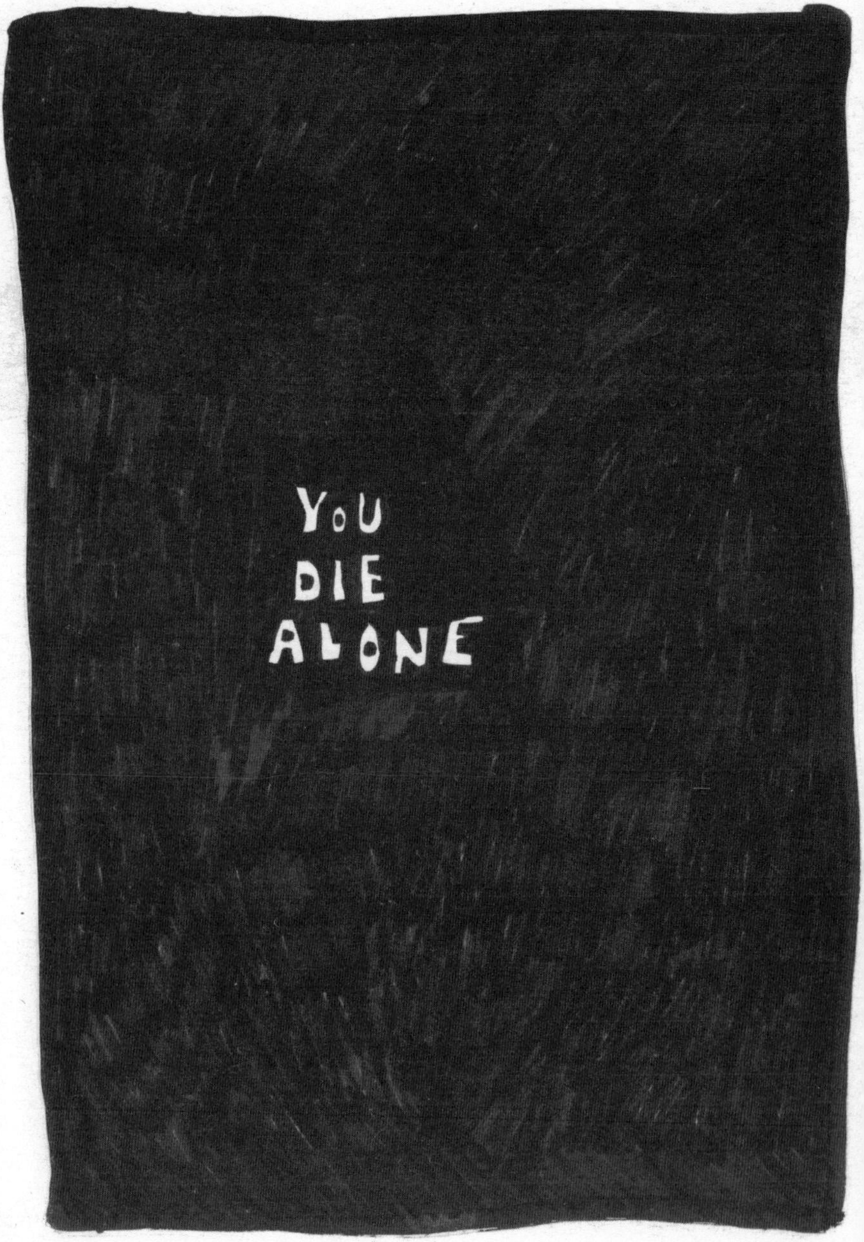
YOU
DIE
ALONE

YOU
STILL
DIE
ALONE

HEY! YOU ARE ON FIRE!

TO CELEBRATE, SET FIRE TO THIS PAGE!

ENSURE YOU USE AN EFFECTIVE PROPELLANT SUCH AS LIGHTER FLUID OR KEROSENE!

REMEMBER TO DISABLE ALL SMOKE ALARMS AND LOCK AWAY ALL HOSES AND EXTINGUISHERS! OR IT WON'T WORK!

USE THIS PAGE TO WRITE DOWN A SECRET!

ONLY, YOU KNOW, PROBABLY NOT ONE ABOUT KIDS OR ANYTHING. SOMEONE MIGHT PICK IT UP AND READ IT AND IT IS ADMISSABLE IN COURT, AS I'VE FOUND TO MY COST.

USE THIS PAGE TO
WRITE A THREATENING
NOTE TO A NEIGHBOUR
WHO KEEPS LEAVING THEIR
STUPID DICKLESS RAZOR
SCOOTER IN THE COMMUNAL
HALLWAY !

DEAR ASSHOLE,

FILL IN THE RECEIPT FOR YOUR WEEKLY BIG SHOP!

(THERE ARE A FEW CLUES TO HELP YOU)

16 x 11p

(A CARCINOGENIC LAGER FROM A COUNTRY THAT NO LONGER EXISTS)

4p

(1 PLY TOILET PAPER)

64p

(HAIR PAINT)

9 x 4p

(CAT/HUMAN FOOD)

3p

(NIGERIAN QUAVERS)

FREE

(BREAKFAST CEREAL BASED ON THE ONE SHOW)

WRITING A STORY? MAKE IT FROM OLD FASHIONED TIMES! CLICK 'CONTROL' AND 'F' ON YOUR COMPUTER AND CHANGE ALL THE 'THE's TO 'YE's! NOW YOU'VE GOT YOURSELF A PERIOD CLASSIC! THOUGH IF YOUR MAIN CHARACTER IS CALLED 'THERESA' SHE'LL NOW BE 'YERESA'. BUT THAT'S OK! NOW YOU HAVE AN ETHNIC PERIOD CLASSIC!

CHA-CHING!

[THIS PAGE HAS BEEN KEPT BLANK ON PURPOSE]

WRITE ABOUT HOW THAT MAKES YOU FEEL...

FILL IN THIS DAILY
MOVEMENT LOG!

DATE	TIME OF MOVEMENT	DURATION	COLOUR	CONSISTENCY	CELEBRITY RESEMB- LANCE

COMPLETELY APPROPRIATE EXCUSES!

DOING STUFF IS HARD, BUT COMING UP FOR REASONS TO NOT DO STUFF IS EVEN HARDER! FEEL FREE TO USE ANY OF THE FOLLOWING EXCUSES!

I HAVE THE SHITS

I AM HAVING GASTRIC ISSUES

TUMMY TROUBLE

I HAVE FOOD POISONING
(WHICH HAS GIVEN ME THE SHITS)

GUT ROT

DEBILITATING RING STING

THERE HAS BEEN SOME SOILING

SQUITS

BEEN ON THE CRAPPER ALL NIGHT

INDISCRIMINATE POOINGS

I HAVE THE RUNS REAL BAD

I HAVE EVACUATED FIRMLY

THE TROTS HAVE CONSUMED ME

I'M RIDING THE BROWN BUS

COPPED FOR A DODGY MEAT SLICE

SQUIRTED MYSELF INSIDE OUT

GOT THE GOK WANS

PEBBLE DASHING

MAKE A MIX TAPE FOR
SOMEONE SPECIAL IN
YOUR LIFE!

WHY?

SIDE ONE
1. ALEX CHILTON - NO SEX
2. JOHN LENNON - HOW DO YOU SLEEP AT NIGHT?
3. KISS - HATE
4. LITA FORD - HATE
5. GG ALLIN - I HATE PEOPLE
6. GG ALLIN - BITE IT YOU SCUM
7. GG ALLIN - SLAUGHTER HOUSE DEATH CAMP
8. CANNIBAL CORPSE - CAULDRON OF HATE
9. SIMPLY RED - HOLDING BACK THE YEARS
10. THE P.G FUCKERS - I HUMP YOUR MOUTH.

SIDE TWO
1. TWELVE MINUTES OF SCREAMING.
2. THEME FROM 'TO CATCH A PREDATOR'
3. EIGHT RANDOM SONGS BY SHALAMAR
4. SEGMENT FROM THE BOOK ON TAPE OF 'WITHOUT REMORSE' BY TOM CLANCY AS READ BY TOM BOSLEY
5. SHAGGY - IT WASN'T ME
6. DAVE MATTHEWS - I DID IT
7. KENNY G. - TOO DRUNK TO FUCK
8. PHIL COLLINS - SUSSUDIO
9. PHIL COLLINS - SUSSUDIO
10. THE DOORS - THE END.

GO TO ONE OF THOSE 'PAINT YOUR OWN POTTERY' PLACES AND RECREATE THE SCENE FROM GHOST WITH A PASSING TRANSIENT!

NEW SWEARS!

HERE ARE SOME NEW RUDE WORDS! JUST SUPPLY THE DEFINITION!

CLEDGE _____

QUINTNER _____

BLINCH HOLE _____

ANDIAN FLUTE PILOT _____

MAMBA JAMBA _____

FLITCHING _____

BOZZLE _____

KLITCH KLAMPING _____

BUBLE _____

I AM A ~~WRITTER~~ PAINTER AND SO CAN YOU BE TOO!

" REMEMBER, YOU ARE NEVER TOO OLD, OR TOO FRENCH, TO GO SOMEWHERE SUNNY AND START PAINTING LADIES WITH THEIR TOPS OFF"

PAUL "PAINTING" GAUGUIN.

TIME TO WRITE YOUR CONFESSION!

DEAR _____,

    I AM SORRY THAT I SMEARED _____ ALL OVER YOUR _____ AND THEN BLAMED IT ON THE _____. I HONESTLY THOUGHT YOU WOULD NEVER _____ MY _____ EVER AGAIN IF YOU KNEW ABOUT MY FREQUENT _____ SOILINGS. I AM NOW GETTING HELP FROM DR. _____ NESSBAUM AND EVERYONE AT THE _____ MEDICAL FACILITY. THE 1000 mg OF _____ TAKEN _____ TIMES A DAY IS HAVING THE DESIRED EFFECT.

    YOURS IN _____, _____

ADD A HILARIOUS SLOGAN TO THE PAINFULLY IRONIC OVER-PRICED T-SHIRT!

WORDS YOU MIGHT WANT TO INCLUDE:
"INSPECTOR" "BEER" "HOT" "HORNY" "KISS"
"TITS" "NIGHT" "BUTT" "UP" "BOOBS" "LOVE"
"MACHINE" "TURDS" "BOB MARLEY" "FART" "FARTS"
"SMELLS" "DRUNK" "GUT" "KNOCKERS" "NERFECT"
"POBOOY'S" "MILF" "GILF" "WTF" "FBI"
"BABY" "KALE" "SPERM" "GASSY" "RAMONES"

WANT TO SOUND INSPIRED?

JUST START A FEW SENTENCES USING THESE HANDY PHRASES:

"HEY! NOW HERE'S A THING..."

"THAT'S INTERESTING, BUT HAVE YOU CONSIDERED THIS..?"

"HMMM, I THINK YOU MIGHT BE MISSING THE POINT THERE..."

"I'M NOT BEING RUDE, I JUST THINK YOU'RE CONFUSED..."

"WHY DO YOU IMMEDIATELY BRING LOOKS INTO IT..?"

"IT WASN'T MY UNCLE THAT GOT DONE FOR FRAUD..."

"OW, STOP THAT OW..."

"LOOK, I'M SORRY, PLEASE PUT THAT DOWN.."

"HELLO?. POLICE?. PLEASE HELP ME..."

I AM A WRITER AND SO CAN YOU BE TOO!

"WHENEVER I WRITE SOMETHING THAT DOESN'T MAKE SENSE OR IS A BIT SHIT, I JUST STICK A FOOTNOTE NEXT TO IT! I KNOW THAT THE READER WILL ASSUME THERE'S SOME KIND OF EXPLANATION THERE, BUT WILL ALMOST CERTAINLY BE TOO LAZY TO READ IT. IT'S SO EASY AND WORKS REALLY WELL WITH STUPID PEOPLE[1]"

-DAVID FOSTER "INFINITE JEST" WALLACE

1. LIKE THIS ONE HERE! DID YOU BOTHER READING IT? I DOUBT IT, BUT JUST IN CASE.[2]

2. HOW ABOUT THIS ONE? TIRED OF THIS YET? LOOK MAN, I'M CRAZY, I CAN FOOTNOTE ALL THE LIVE LONG DAY. DON'T BELIEVE ME?[3]

3. YOU SEE?

LOOK OUT! THIS PAGE IS HAUNTED (
WOOOOOOOOOOOOOOOOOOOOOOOOO HI

(NOTE TO EDITOR: CHRIST I DON'T KNOW, MAYBE STICK
A PICTURE OF A GHOST ON HERE OR SOMETHING. BUT
NOT IF THE DESIGNER SAYS IT WILL TAKE A WEEK
AND COST 3K. JUST STEAL SOMETHING OFF THE
INTERNET IF THEY PULL THAT SHIT. OR I'LL FUCKING
DO IT. JESUS, I AM SO OVER THIS THING. I CAN
FEEL IT SUCKING THE SOUL OUT OF MY
BODY. DO YOU KNOW MY NOVEL GOT REJECTED
AGAIN? UNBELIEVABLE. 'A NICE REJECTION'
MY AGENT SAID. 'MIGHT BE TOO GOOD FOR
US.' CAN YOU BELIEVE IT? IF IT'S THAT
FUCKING GOOD, WHY WOULDN'T YOU PUBLISH
IT? I REALLY FEEL LIKE KILLING
MYSELF. HONESTLY. I MIGHT DO IT
THIS TIME. ASSHOLES.]

RECONNECT WITH YOUR INNER CHILD!
*SWEAR INDISCRIMINATELY!
*BULLY THOSE DIFFERENT THAN YOU!
*LITTER!
*WEAR CONFUSING TROUSERS!
*TALK IN THAT ANNOYING WAY!
*HAVE POOR POSTURE!
*FRIGHTEN THE ELDERLY!
*RUIN EVERYTHING!

COVER THE BACK OF THIS LAVATORY DOOR WITH SMEARS, FILTH AND HORRIBLY OFFENSIVE GRAFFITI!

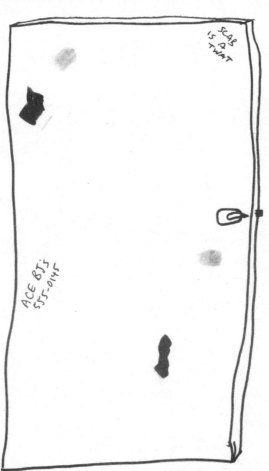

AT THIS VERY MOMENT IN TIME I AM ...

SMELLING LIKE _____

SKULKING BEHIND SOME _____ BY THE
                              YOGA STUDIO

TOUCHING MYSELF AND THINKING OF _____
                    FROM THE ANTIQUES ROADSHOW

EATING A MICROWAVABLE _____

ENTIRELY CAKED IN _____

LUMBERED WITH THE NICKNAME _____
        DUE TO MY CONSTANT _____

SWEATING IN _____ PARTS OF MY BODY.

COUGHING UP _____

HIDING IN THE TOILET DUE TO CONSTANT THREATS
                    FROM THE _____

UNNERVING MY LOCAL _____ DUE TO MY
        INSISTENCE ON WEARING _____

THREATENING _____

[THIS PAGE HAS BEEN KEPT BLANK ON PURPOSE]

WRITE ABOUT HOW THAT MAKES YOU FEEL...

WORD SEARCHING!

THE GRID BELOW FEATURES A NUMBER OF NON-INSPIRATIONAL MESSAGES. YOU MUST VEHEMENTLY SCORE THEM OUT TO PROVOKE POSITIVE INSPIRATION! AND AS I HAVE NO FAITH IN YOUR ABILITIES, I HAVE LEFT OUT ALL THOSE TROUBLESOME EXTRA LETTERS. ENJOY!

PEST (SEXUAL)

BUMBLING DOLT

ANUS

FAILURE EPITOMISED

PALE IMITATION OF JAMES MAY

TITTYFUCKWAD

TALENTLESS PRICK

OWNS STINGAL BVM

JAMIROQUAI

JARAG

PRISSCVM

YOU SUCK

SMELLS

FINGERS STRAY CATS

SOC

FUVK

FARTKNOCKER

HEY! AN INK BLOT TEST!

[TELL ME WHAT YOU SEE IN THE STAIN!]

GUESSES HERE: _____

[THIS PAGE HAS BEEN KEPT BLANK ON PURPOSE]

WRITE ABOUT HOW THAT MAKES YOU FEEL...

GO OUTSIDE AND HIDE THIS BOOK IN A TREE!

IF I MAY SUGGEST, THERE'S A GREAT TREE IN THE BACK GARDEN OF THE BUNGALOW AT 11 WELLINGTON TERRACE. THERE'S QUITE A LOW FENCE. AND IF YOU CAN WRITE SOMETHING IN THE BOOK ALONG THE LINES OF 'CAROL, HOW COULD YOU?' OR 'I WILL BE WATCHING YOU ALWAYS.' TRY TO MAKE A BIT OF NOISE WHILE YOU'RE DOING IT. DISRUPT A COUPLE OF HANGING BASKETS. MAKE SURE THEY KNOW SOMEONE'S BEEN THERE.

INVENT A NEW ANIMAL!

DRAW IT!

NAME IT!   "KANGAMOOSE"

NOW THINK ABOUT WHY YOU ARE
      DOING THIS AND WHAT'S
GONE WRONG WITH YOUR LIFE!

WRITE ABOUT HOW THAT MAKES YOU FEEL.

HERE'S SOME DENIM HOT PANTS AND A BEJEWELLING GUN! YOU KNOW WHAT TO DO!

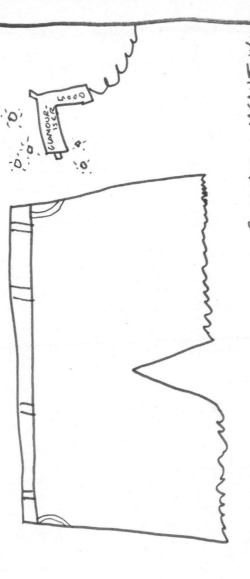

[ACTUALLY YOU PROBABLY DON'T, DO YOU? WHAT I MEANT WAS DECORATE THE HOT PANTS. STILL TOO COMPLICATED? YOU MAKE SHORT SHORTS GO NICE. DOES THAT WORK? OR SHOULD I TRY A SERIES OF GRUNTS?]

LOOK, IF YOU'RE
AN ARTIST, WEAR
A BERET

OTHERWISE
YOU CAN
JUST FUCK
OFF

SIT OUTSIDE THE WINDOW OF
A FANCY RESTAURANT AND STARE
OPEN-MOUTHED AT THE DINERS.
WRITE DOWN WHAT THEY SCREAM
AT YOU!

GIVE YOURSELF A PAT!

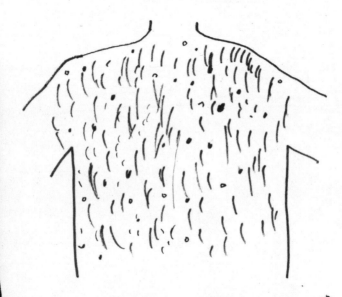

ON THE BACK!

[YOU MIGHT WANT TO WASH YOUR HANDS AFTERWARDS]

I AM A WRITER AND SO CAN YOU BE TOO!

"I HONESTLY BELIEVE THAT CHILDREN ARE THE FUTURE AND IF YOU TEACH THEM WELL, LET THEM LEAD THE WAY AND ALWAYS SHOW THEM ALL THE BEAUTY THEY POSSESS INSIDE WHILE STILL GIVING THEM THE SENSE OF PRIDE TO MAKE IT EASIER THEN THAT CHILDREN'S LAUGHTER WILL REMIND US HOW WE USED TO BE. AND, IN A WAY, THAT IS THE GREATEST LOVE OF ALL."

MAHATMA "PEACE" GANDHI

HEY! WHY NOT DRAW YOUR SPIRIT
ANIMAL DOWN BELOW!

⬇   ⬇

OR IF YOU'RE NOT INSANE OR LIVING
IN SOME BIZARRE TIME-WASTING
WONDERLAND YOU COULD DO SOMETHING
USEFUL LIKE HELP A DEAF PERSON
OR PICK UP SOME LITTER OR SOMETHING.

FILL IN THE PASSIVE AGGRESSIVE TEXT MESSAGE EXCHANGE!

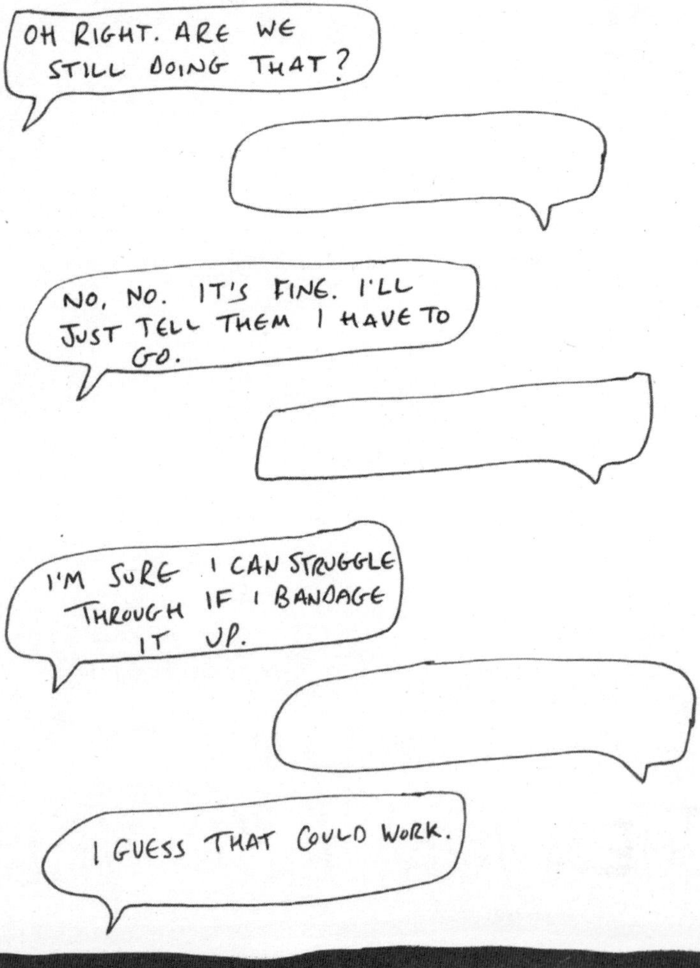

BRANDISH THIS BOOK THREATENINGLY IN THE FACE OF AN ELDERLY SECURITY GUARD!

THEN RUN LIKE HELL!

FEELING BESIEGED?

YOU CAN TURN THIS BOOK INTO A FORT!*

JUST
PILE
'EM
ON
UP!

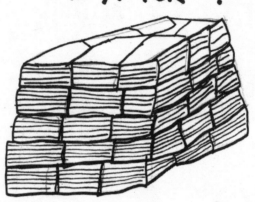

*[CONSTRUCTION OF A BOOK FORT WILL REQUIRE PURCHASE OF AN ADDITIONAL 16 COPIES OF THIS BOOK. ONLY THIS BOOK CAN BE USED IN THE CONSTRUCTION OF A BOOK FORT. ADDITIONAL BOOKS CAN BE PURCHASED FROM THE FOLLOWING RETAILERS: AMAZON, W.H. SMITH, WATERSTONES, PLAY.COM, TESCO. DO NOT PURCHASE ADDITIONAL BOOK FORT BOOKS FROM AN INDEPENDENT RETAILER, THEY OFFER LESS OF A KICK-BACK TO US. ADDITIONAL COPIES ARE PROHIBITED TO BE PASSED ON AS GIFTS. THIS IS ILLEGAL UNDER EU LAW. THE AUTHOR AND PUBLISHER ALWAYS PROSECUTES.]

I AM A WRITER AND SO CAN YOU BE TOO!

"WEARING BIG THICK GLASSES IS A REALLY GOOD WAY OF LOOKING DEAD DEAD BRAINY. BEFORE I GOT A PAIR, LOADS OF PEOPLE THOUGHT I WAS THICK AS SHIT. BUT A QUICK TRIP TO SPEESAVERS — BISH, BASH BOSH — AND I NEARLY GOT A NOBEL PRIZE. NOT TOO SHABBY."

JEAN 'NAUSEA' PAUL SATRE.

NEVER FORGET

IF ALL ELSE
FAILS, YOU
CAN ALWAYS

RUN AWAY

SEEKING INSPIRATION? FRENCH MAVERICK MARCEL PROUST SAID, "SMELLS ARE AS GOOD AT INSPIRING STUFF AS LOOKING AT STUFF." THIS FAMOUS PHRASE HAS BECOME A VITAL COG IN EVERY CREATIVE PERSON'S TOOL BOX. SIT FOR A MOMENT. NOW SNIFF. PERHAPS YOU CAN SMELL TOAST? DOES IT REMIND YOU OF CRISPY CHILDHOOD MORNINGS? FULL OF WONDER AND MEALS? IS SOMEONE MAKING TOAST? IF THEY'RE NOT, YOU MIGHT BE HAVING A STROKE. FEEL YOUR FACE. IS IT NUMB? OH GOD, I THINK YOU'RE HAVING A STROKE. OK, DON'T PANIC. STOP BEING INSPIRED AND ALERT THE NECESSARY AUTHORITIES. THERE ISN'T MUCH TIME. NO, WAIT, IT IS TOAST. PHEW, THANK GOODNESS. YOU CAN SEE YOUR WIFE THROUGH THE HATCH MAKING YOU SOME DELICIOUS HOT BREAD AS A TREAT. MAYBE THE SMELL REMINDS YOU OF A LONG LOST HOLIDAY. POSSIBLY IN A CARAVAN IF YOUR FROM THAT SORT OF FAMILY. OH, HOLD ON. DIDN'T YOUR WIFE DIE FOUR YEARS AGO? OK, I'M PRETTY SURE THIS IS A STROKE-INSPIRED HALLUCINATION. IS THERE A BURNING SENSATION UNDER YOUR SKULL? YES, I KNOW YOU CAN SMELL TOAST, FORGET THE TOAST. YOU ARE DYING. YOU ARE GOING TO DIE. CONTACT A MEDICAL PROFESSIONAL. I CAN'T STRESS ENOUGH, IF YOU ARE SMELLING TOAST FOR PROUSTIAN INSPIRATION AND NO TOAST IS PRESENT, THEN THIS IS A SIGNATURE SYMPTOM OF A STROKE. TRY TO MAKE PASSERS-BY AWARE OF THE SITUATION USING YOUR DAMAGED, FLOPPY MOUTH AND LIPS TO REPLICATE SOME KIND OF DISTRESSED NOISE. DO YOU WANT TO BE A VEGETABLE? DO YOU WANT AN UNDER PAID EASTERN EUROPEAN WOMAN WIPING YOUR ARSE AND MAKING YOU SOUP? THAT'S A STROKE MY FRIEND. WRITE ABOUT HOW THAT MAKES YOU FEEL. ⟹

HERE'S A FRAME! DRAW
A SELF-PORTRAIT!

THAT'S GREAT!

AND AS A TITLE CAN I
SUGGEST
"SELF-DELUSION"

BELLOW! BELLOW NOISES OF JOY!

UNICYCLING!

JUGGLING!

FIRE POI !

TUMBLING!

STILT WALKING!

DIABOLO !

NONE OF THESE THINGS ARE CONSIDERED
CREATIVE. AVOID.

COLOUR ME IN!
[EVEN THOUGH I'M AN ADULT!]
"THE GHOST OF DENNIS HOPPER WITH A CHICKEN MANGO SALSA WRAP"

GOT A FUNKY BASEBALL CAP?

COOL!

WHY NOT WEAR IT BACKWARDS TO COMPLETELY REINFORCE YOUR INDIVIDUALITY!

STAND ON ONE LEG!

THEN THINK ABOUT ALL THE PEOPLE IN THE WORLD WHO ARE LESS FORTUNATE THAN YOU. THEIR HARDSHIP. THEIR STRUGGLE. WHAT ARE YOU DOING FOR THEM? OH I SEE, STANDING ON ONE LEG. GREAT. THAT'LL CURE MALARIA.

WRITE ABOUT HOW THAT MAKES YOU FEEL

DON'T JUST BE CREATIVE...
ALSO BE CREAT-HIVE!

1. FIND A BEEHIVE!

2. PUNCH ALL THE BEES IN THE FACE!

3. USE THEIR ANGER AND STINGING TO INSPIRE A STORY ABOUT BEES!

HERE'S THE THICK MUSCULAR NECK OF A BOUNCER FROM DONCASTER CALLED STEVE!
WHY NOT FILL IT IN WITH APPROPRIATE TATTOOS!

I AM A WRITER AND SO CAN YOU BE TOO!

"Look, writing is just like taking a shit. You sit down, you concentrate, you strain, you sweat and if there isn't any blood in it, you're not doing it right."
JANE "MR. DARCY" AUSTEN

WRITE ABOUT HOW THAT MAKES YOU FEEL.

DRAW A PICTURE OF THE DREAM YOU HAD LAST NIGHT!

CHRIST KNOWS IT'S BETTER THAN ACTUALLY HEARING ABOUT IT.

REVENGE IS A LIFE WELL LIVED!

THOUGH THAT PROBABLY WON'T APPLY TO YOU — SO MAYBE BUY SOME NUMCHUCKS OR SOMETHING...

LEAVE THIS PAGE OUT
IN THE SUN AND
LET IT FADE!

(JUST LIKE ALL YOUR
PARENTS' HOPES FOR
YOU FADED WHEN YOU
DROPPED OUT OF AIR CONDITIONER
REPAIR SCHOOL AND STARTED
LISTENING TO REGGAE
ALL THE TIME)

ADD CREATIVITY TO EVERY ASPECT OF YOUR LIFE!

- DON'T JUST MAKE A SANDWICH — DO SOME SLAM POETRY AS YOU MAKE A SANDWICH!

- DON'T JUST STEAL A CATERING PACK OF SWEETENER FROM WORK — PERFORM AN INTERPRETIVE DANCE AS YOU STEAL A CATERING PACK OF SWEETENER FROM WORK!

- DON'T ILLEGALLY FLY TIP AN OLD SET OF KITCHEN CABINETS AT A COUNTRY PARK — MAKE UP A HIP-HOP RAP AS YOU ILLEGALLY FLY TIP AN OLD SET OF KITCHEN CABINETS AT A COUNTRY PARK!

DON'T JUST SOB UNCONTROLLABLY — SOB UNCONTROLLABLY OVER A PREPARED CANVAS AND MAKE SOME ART!

TURN THAT FROWN UPSIDE DOWN!

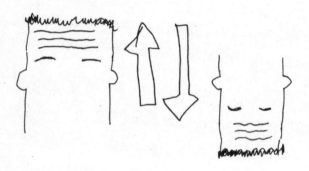

ACTUALLY, NO. DON'T DO THAT. IT LOOKS HIDEOUS. HAVE YOU CONSIDERED BOTOX? OR VEILS ARE BIG THIS YEAR?

CRANK TH'S PAGE UP TO ELEVEN!

[WHICH ALSO HAPPENS TO BE THE EMOTIONAL AGE OF ANYONE WHO ACTUALLY SAYS THAT KIND OF THING.]

I JUST WANTED TO SAY YOU ARE ABSOLUTELY AMAZING...!!!

OH...WAIT...No, I MUST HAVE BEEN MIXING YOU UP WITH SOMEONE ELSE. A FRIEND OF MINE WHO'S ABSOLUTELY AMAZING + HAS GOT THAT SAME CARDIGAN.

I'M NOT SAYING YOU
SHOULD USE THIS PAGE
AS A MAKESHIFT WANK Sock.

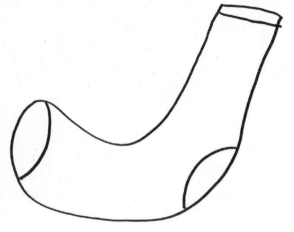

I'M JUST SAYING THAT YOU
COULD USE THIS PAGE
AS A MAKESHIFT WANK Sock.

[THIS PAGE HAS BEEN KEPT
BLANK ON PURPOSE]

WRITE ABOUT HOW THAT MAKES YOU FEEL...

HERE IS THE CALENDAR

M	T	W
1. HAVE BENEFITS STOPPED	2. ACCUSATIONS OF IMPROPRIETY	3. SCRAPE MOSS FROM WINDOWS
8. GENERAL RIDICULE (PEERS)	9. GET MISTAKEN FOR JOHN SERGEANT (4 PM)	10. EJECTED FROM SOFT PLAY AREA
15. SHAME	16. SHOW PHARMACIST YOUR LUMP	17. FLEE FROM BAILIFFS
22. LAUGHING IRONICALLY	23. APPEARANCE ON EGGHEADS	24. BUY SWEATPANTS
29. OUTWITTED BY CROWS	30. BREATHING DIFFICULTIES	31. LOSE ALL HOPE

FOR THE REST OF YOUR LIFE!

T	F	S	S
4. COUGHING	5. LEARN TRUTH ABOUT PARENTAGE	6. CHOKE ON BUDGET NUGGETS	7. CRYING
11. ITCHING	12. COMICAL SUICIDE ATTEMPT	13. TAKE A TUMBLE IN THE COVERED MARKET	14. CRYING
18. GET DRUNK ON CORSODYL	19. FIDDLE WITH SELF (2-7)	20. HURT	21. CRYING
25. CHRISTMAS	26. MOCKED BY TEENS (BUS STOP)	27. SOIL YOURSELF (BUS STOP)	28. CRYING (BUS STOP)
1. DARKNESS	2. GLOOM	3. MURK	4. CRYING

- SHAKE THIS BOOK'S HAND!
- HUG THIS BOOK!
- GIVE THIS BOOK A PLAYFUL KISS!
- TAKE THIS BOOK ON A DATE!
- GET SERIOUS WITH THIS BOOK!
- MOVE INTO THIS BOOK'S FLAT!
- PROPOSE TO THIS BOOK!
- GET MARRIED TO THIS BOOK!
- HAVE ONE WONDERFUL CHILD WITH THIS BOOK AND ONE EVIL LITTLE SHIT!
- NOTICE THIS BOOK IS SUDDENLY 'GOING OUT' A LOT!
- REALISE THIS BOOK IS DELETING ITS BROWSER HISTORY A LOT!
- FOLLOW THIS BOOK!
- CONFRONT THIS BOOK!
- HAVE THIS BOOK LEAVE YOU FOR A MAN WHO DOES CAR BOOT SALES FOR A LIVING. NO, HONESTLY, CAR BOOT SALES!
- STARE AT THIS BOOK THROUGH THE WINDOW!

RIP OUT THIS PAGE!
THEN RETURN THE BOOK TO THE POINT OF PURCHASE FOR A FULL REFUND. SAY SOMETHING LIKE, "EXCUSE ME, I JUST GOT THIS BOOK BUT THERE'S A PAGE RIPPED OUT OF IT." DON'T WAVE THE RIPPED PAGE AT THEM WHILE SAYING IT. KEEP YOUR STORY STRAIGHT. DON'T GO INTO TOO MUCH DETAIL. DON'T OVER-COMPLICATE IT. NICE AND SIMPLE. IF THEY START TO GET SUSPICIOUS OR REACH FOR A PHONE OR SAY THEY NEED TO REFER IT UPSTAIRS, THROW PEPPER IN THEIR FACE AND RUN. GO FOR THE EYES. DON'T LEAVE THE BOOK BEHIND (FINGERPRINTS).

MAYBE YOU CAN WRITE A POEM ABOUT IT OR SOMETHING.

ON THIS PAGE WRITE A
SONG ABOUT WHAT YOU
♪ DID TODAY! ♫

AND REMEMBER LOADS OF
WORDS RHYME WITH "SOB",
"CRY" AND "WEEP" BUT HARDLY
ANYTHING RHYMES WITH "ANGRILY
SELF-ABUSING WHILE EATING SOUP"

DON'T FORGET!
YOU CAN'T SPELL

INSPIRATION

WITHOUT
'RATION'!

[NOT REALLY THOUGHT THIS ONE THROUGH.
MAYBE 'RATION OUT YOUR IDEAS'? THAT
DOESN'T REALLY MAKE SENSE. I CAN'T IMAGINE YOU
HAVE THAT MANY IDEAS, SO FOR GOD'S SAKE DON'T RATION
THEM. MAYBE 'RATION THE TERRIBLE IDEAS'? YEAH
THAT'LL DO. IT MEANS THAT.]

WATCH OUT!

THIS PAGE IS
TICKLISH!

TEE HEE HEE

TEE HEE HEE

TEE HEE
FUCKING
HEE.

(I AM 43 YEARS OLD)

DANCE LIKE NOBODY'S WATCHING!
EXCEPT GOD AND JESUS OBVIOUSLY.
GOD AND JESUS ARE ALWAYS WATCHING.
AND ALWAYS JUDGING.
YOU CANNOT ESCAPE THE JUDGEMENT
OF OUR LORD JESUS CHRIST.
PRAISE HIM! PRAISE HIM!
LET THE HOLY SPIRIT
ENGULF YOU AND
SAVE YOU

LET'S PLAY "YOUR INEVITABLE DECLINE" BINGO!
COLLAPSE OF PERSONAL HYGIENE!
YOUR BEST FRIENDS ARE CRUMBS!
SMALL CHILDREN MOCK YOU AT BUS STOPS!
YOU USE THE WORD 'SMEARED' A LOT!
NEIGHBOURS COMPLAIN ABOUT YOUR BREATHING!
YOUR PETS CRY!
IS THAT SMELL YOU? OR SOMETHING YOU'VE FORGOTTEN?
A DISEASE IS NAMED AFTER YOU!
FOUR MEALS A DAY HAVE HAM IN THEM!
BIRTHDAY SPENT IN CUSTODY!
YOU LOVINGLY STROKE A MACHETE THAT YOU'VE NAMED 'JUSTICE'!
YOU START PLAYING BINGO!

WHAT WILL YOUR LAST WORDS BE?

(CIRCLE THE MOST LIKELY CANDIDATE!)

"DON'T BE STUPID, COUGARS DON'T BITE."

"IS FIRE EDIBLE?"

"AAAA GGGGG GG HHHHHHHHHHHH"

"WHAT'S THAT HOVERCRAFT DOING?"

"THAT'S NOT EVEN A REAL MACHETE..."

"HOW DOES THE RHYME GO? IS IT 'WINE BEFORE LIGHTER FLUID FEELING FINE'?"

"DON'T WORRY, I'LL GO AND TALK TO HIM."

"WWWW AAA AAA AAHHHHHH HHH HHH"

"HEY EVERYONE! LOOK AT ME!"

"THIS TAKES ME BACK."

"WAGER ACCEPTED!"

"NVVVVV VVVVV VVV VVVV VV VVVVVVVVVH"

"WHAT DOES THIS LEVER DO?"

"HOT YOGA? SIGN ME UP!"

"I HATE YOU ALL."

"SSSSSHHHHHH III TTTBBBAA LLLLLLLS"

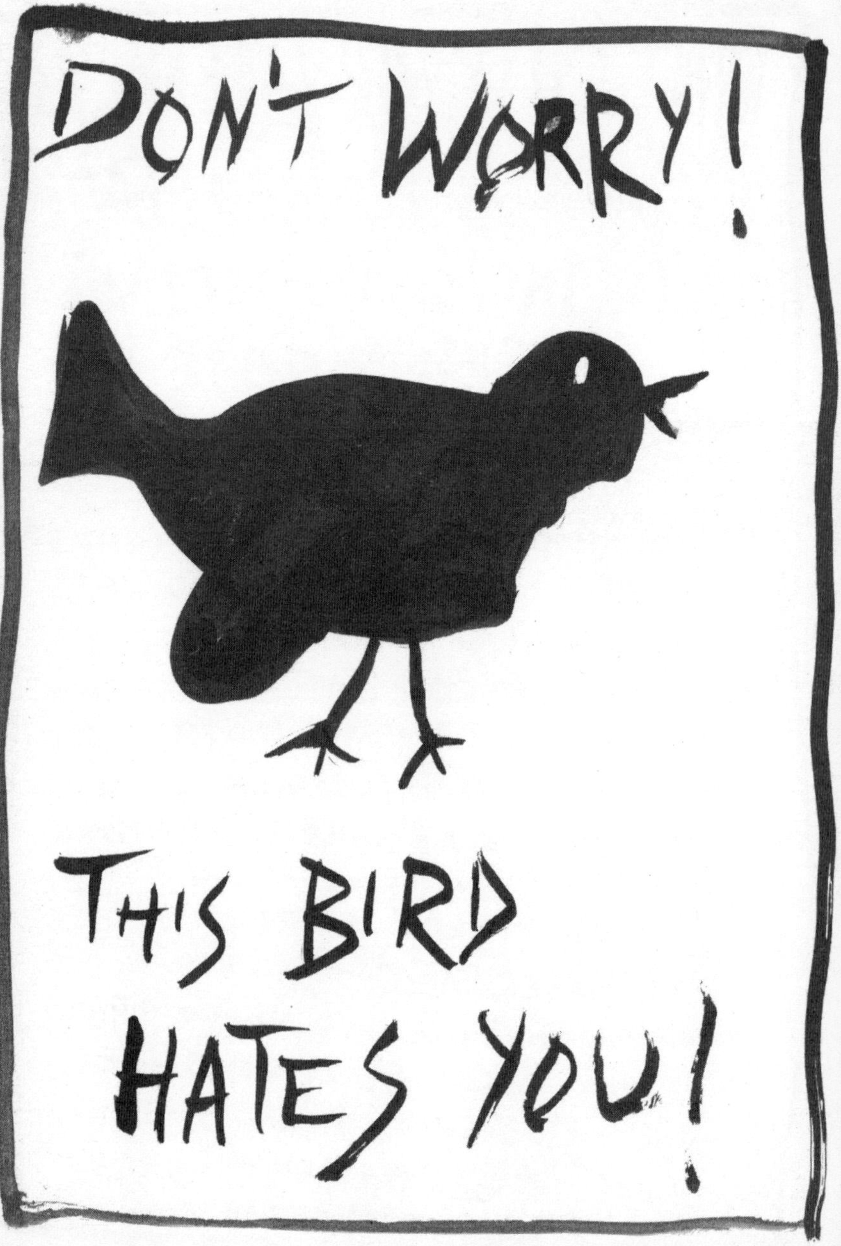
DON'T WORRY!
THIS BIRD
HATES YOU!

TRY TO KNOCK THE COWBOY'S HAT OFF!

(NO, I HAVE NO IDEA HOW YOU CAN POSSIBLY ACHIEVE THIS EITHER. I MAY HAVE REACHED MY LOWEST EBB. IT'S 4.23 AM, MY DEADLINE IS LOOMING AND ALL I'VE DONE IS THIS PAGE AND TWO OTHERS WHICH ARE EVEN MORE SHIT. I'D KILL MYSELF BUT I CAN'T AFFORD THAT MUCH PARACETAMOL)

WOW! IT'S A GREAT BIG EMPTY SPACE!

NEARLY REACHED MY MINIMUM PAGE COUNT!

NEVER GIVE UP!
NEVER EVER GIVE UP!
NEVER EVER EVER
GIVE UP!
NEVER EVER EVER EVER
GIVE UP!
NEVER EVER

OH LOOK! IT'S YOUR TOMBSTONE!
FILL IT IN WITH ALL THE GORY DETAILS!

NOW TAKE ALL
I HAVE TAUGHT
YOU AND...
CHANGE THE
WORLD!

YEAH. RIGHT.

THANKS:
LUCY, JAMIE, RICHARD, CLAUDIA, OLLIE, LUCINDA, GRACE, ED, STEVE, MADELEINE, WILL, RICHARD, SCOTT, RON.

NO THANKS:
CAROL.